Binary Trading

Profitable strategies for binary betting

by John Piper

HARRIMAN HOUSE LTD
3A Penns Road
Petersfield
Hampshire
GU32 2EW
GREAT BRITAIN

Tel: +44 (0)1730 233870
Fax: +44 (0)1730 233880
Email: enquiries@harriman-house.com
Website: www.harriman-house.com

First published in Great Britain in 2009 by Harriman House.

Copyright © Harriman House Ltd

The right of John Piper to be identified as the author has been asserted
in accordance with the Copyright, Design and Patents Act 1988.

Charts © IG Index, Tenfore and Updata.

ISBN 978-1-905641-71-0

British Library Cataloguing in Publication Data
A CIP catalogue record for this book can be obtained from the British Library.

Printed in the UK by the MPG Books Group

This book is for all those traders out there looking for an edge!

Contents

Appendices

Biography

John has been trading markets since the mid '80s, mainly writing options but also trading futures. The highlights have been trading right through the '87 Crash (mainly selling put options – hence the lack of hair!), annual turnover exceeding £2m of option premiums on his personal account, managing money in excess of $1m, winning a TV trading contest and generally spending far too much time glued to screens. Whilst abusing himself in this way he also decided to help other traders and started *The Technical Trader* in 1989 and which has become the leading trading newsletter in the UK. *The Technical Trader* filled a void and the business has helped many traders over the years. The newsletter can now be found on the web.

Over the years John has developed a number of trading techniques; he summarises his approach as *Psycho-Trading* – meaning getting into the mind of the market. John spends his time in the Surrey Hills but makes frequent trips to warmer climes with the Hash House Harriers – a club for those who like a drink but who have a running problem!

John runs two market services and one of these exclusively covers binary betting.

Other books by John Piper:

The Way to Trade

The Fortune Strategy

Financial Cataclysm Now!

Binary Betting

If you would like to receive John's free news sheet send a blank email to jptt@aweber.com

The author welcomes feedback and can be contacted at:

john@john-piper.com; his website is www.johnpiper.info

Preface

Who should read this book

- Anyone who has read my **introductory guide to binary betting** and wants to know more. The first book was written to explain the basics of binary bets – this one goes a whole lot further!

- Those who have been **struggling with spread betting**, or other forms of betting and trading, who want to find a better way.

- **Experienced traders** will also find a lot of value within these pages. I have traded futures and options for 20 years and there are some very good reasons why I now use binary bets.

- Those who **do not like paying commissions**.

- Those who **do not like paying tax** – because your profits from binary bets will be tax free!

Why you need this book

I am writing this advanced book to follow on from where my earlier book, *Binary Betting*, left off. The earlier book was specifically designed as an introductory guide accessible to experts and novices alike. This second book assumes some knowledge but only as much as you can get from reading the first book. Binary bets offer those who bet on sporting events and trade financial markets some of the best deals available. In this book I am going to take you on a ride through my trading approach and through many trades I have done myself.

Let me give you one example which goes to the heart of why binary bets are so attractive. Chapter 5 is all about *trading the news*. Most traders run a mile when the news comes out as it can produce sharp moves in both directions, albeit not usually at the same time, but with markets as they were in October 2008 even that would have been no surprise! But with binary bets we welcome the news as a great profit opportunity. Our risk is 100% controlled and the sharp moves which we often see when the news comes out are like a gift from heaven for the binary trader.

Of course you have to choose the right bets. Read on…

Whatever you do in life there is risk and there is a potential reward. When you place a bet you want the maximum reward for the minimum risk. That is a magic formula, a winning formula – and it is a formula which binary bets offer. But only if you handle them correctly – this book tells you how to do just that.

How this book is structured

The first chapter kicks off with a "Day in the Life". In the text I say it was tough but I spent that particular day trading from the tropical paradise that is Phuket and making a decent profit – it does not get much better than that! (I very much enjoy trading and I also very much enjoy tropical paradises. I see no reason at all not to combine the two.) In this chapter I explain why I took the trades I did and we begin to look at how we can trade the market (FTSE in this case) using binary bets.

In Chapters 2 and 3 we leave practice behind and look at some theory. Chapter 2 is concerned with a number of different approaches to trading the markets with binaries and Chapter 3 looks at some of the key bets and outlines ways in which they can be used.

Those three chapters comprise Part I of the book and we then move onto Part II – the Strategies.

In part II we learn how to trade:

- **longer-term** bets with a maximum of six months duration
- the **news**
- the **waves** (Elliott Wave Theory)
- the **spikes** (Market Profile)
- the **mind of the market**
- **trendlines and moving averages**

Part III is a critical part of this book and explains how you, as a human being, interact with the market and how to develop your trading approach.

Part III also includes a lot of essential information on statistics – stuff traders need to know in order to survive.

Finally, in the Appendices you will find a wealth of material to back up some of the key information in this book, including the 5 point trading plan – something that may inspire you!

Introduction

Little more than a year ago I wrote *Binary Betting* – an introduction to binary betting. At the time my publisher had to hold me back. Explaining how binaries work is clearly an essential thing to do. But my passion is trading and it is the trading of binaries that really interests me.

Don't get me wrong, *Binary Betting* is a great book and was the first book written about this important new way of trading. I was not the first trader to discover binary bets, by a long way, but I am proud that I was the first to share it with other traders.

But as I was writing *Binary Betting* my publisher kept reassuring me. "Don't worry," he would say, "once people understand the basics you can write the book you want to. Just stick to the basics this time."

Well, it was a long, hard grind but we got it done.

And now I have written the book I wanted – *here it is*!

In this book you will find that binaries come alive rather like a Porsche 911 in the hands of a good driver. No longer will you be at the whim of the market, a few ticks away from hitting your stop, but you can trade the most outrageous moves in complete safety. I am not saying you will always win but you can plan your strategy in the knowledge that you will never, bar a few exceptions, get stopped out and that you can only risk what you put down on the table.

Today in the UK over 70% of adults get involved in some form of gambling and trading. At the same time we have more opportunities to gamble and bet than ever before. It is estimated that around four million Britons take part in the £5.25 billion online gambling business.

This book is about a relatively small sector within the online gaming business. Binary bets, as we know them now, were only introduced in 2003, but they offer many benefits over other forms of betting and trading. Here is a brief summary of those benefits. Only one of these is exclusive to binary bets, but no other form of betting offers the same powerful combination:

- the ability to bet on both sporting events and financial markets
- fixed-odds betting allowing tight control of risk

- constantly updated prices which can move very quickly

- the option of opening a bet at any time

- the option of closing a bet at any time – you don't have to wait until the game is over

- low minimum bets so you can cut your teeth without risking the ranch

- high maximum bets so you can rake it in once you know what you are doing

- the ability to place bets on the internet, via suitably equipped mobile phones (PDAs), and (sometimes) by telephone

- the availability of some unique bets giving unrivalled flexibility

If you are looking for fun, rather than cash, then this book will show you how to have fun in a way that will also give you a good chance of making money. But there will be times when you have to choose between fun and cash – you can't always have both.

Part I – Essentials

1.

A Day in the Life of a FTSE Binaries Trader

The FTSE on 26 November 2007

It's a tough life for us traders

Getting up early to review the charts before FTSE opens can be simply too much bother for some traders but I consider it essential. As I do this I make notes and here are today's:

Date: Monday 26 November 2007
Location: Naithonburi Beach Resort, Phuket
FTSE's prior close: 6262.1
200 day MA: c.6420
Major Trendlines: c.6000 – 6500
Notes: FTSE has bounced well off Thursday's (22nd November) low at 6026.9 – see chart below – and it looks like it is time for a pullback (possible five-wave form developing) so I plan to go short today. The big question at this time is whether this rally is going to build a head of steam into the Christmas period. Elliott Wave patterns suggest two main alternatives. Either a feeble wave 4 rally which could stagger into Christmas, or new impulsive action which would give the bulls some real festive cheer. Either way I expect more upside but FTSE may well want to re-test 6026.9 first – it is this re-test that sets the scene for the trade today.

Right, it is now time for breakfast on the beach. Damn hot it is to – I said it was tough! I have around six hours until FTSE opens and the fun begins, I have to try not to be too miserable in this island paradise up to that point.

As this is titled "a day in the life" I suppose I ought to mention the sunbathing, wave jumping, and lunch...

Actually I will mention lunch.

I ordered king prawns and they were around 12" long! Pretty impressive prawns. And freshly barbequed. It doesn't hurt that they cost around £6 – I would have paid ten times that in the UK, although no restaurant in the UK can compete with a Thai beach for ambience.

Anyway at 2:50pm (7:50am in the frozen wastes) I was back "on station" at my PC expecting an early rally and looking to sell as I think it is time for a pullback.

Market opens

The early action supported my view with a failed break above 6300 (meaning FTSE poked its head above 6300 and promptly fell back) and at this point I bought the following bets:

1. *FTSE to end down >50 points* – bought at 11.4

2. *FTSE cash low to be <-100* – bought at 8.9

Both of these bets should prosper if we see a decent fall, even if FTSE does not go all the way.

I did consider the bet *FTSE to end down* but it was priced at around 40 and this did not offer such good odds. To put this in trading terms the risk/reward was not to my liking.

Here is a chart of the action including the sell signals on the day itself. I have also marked the possible five-waves up on this chart. The five-wave pattern is a technique from the Elliott Wave Theory and I will be discussing and explaining this thoughout the book.

Chart 1.1: FTSE 100 Index, 24-26 Nov 2007

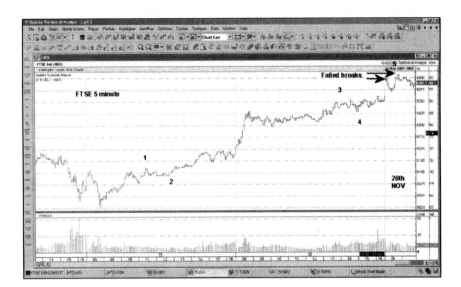

A quick note on binary betting

For those of you unfamiliar with the delights of binary trading I ought to make a number of important points.

Unlike with spread betting I am not worried if I do not catch the high – I cannot get stopped out of most binary bets, even if I wanted to. The fact a market may go 30 or 40 points against me is not of major concern as long as it goes the right way eventually.

If I buy a bet at 40 my maximum profit is 60 (100 – 40) as a binary bet can only move between zero and 100. That is a reward of only 1.5 times my risk (60 divided by 40 = 1.5 = 150%). But consider this ratio on my other two bets. Buying at 11.4 gives me a potential reward of 88.6 (100 – 11.4) and a ratio of almost 8:1. Buying at 8.9 is even better giving a potential reward of 91.1 (100 – 8.9) and a ratio in excess of 10:1.

Consider this in the context of risking a total of £100 on each bet:

- Buying at 11.4 allows £9 per point (11.4 x £9 = £102.60). My maximum potential reward is then £797.40 (88.6 x £9= £797.40). *In percentage terms that is a return of 777%!*

- Buying at 8.9 allows £11 per point (8.9 x £11 = £97.90). My maximum potential reward is then £1002.10 (91.1 x £11= £1002.10). *In percentage terms that is a return of 1023%!*

You will notice that risk/reward is significantly better if we risk less in the first place and the lesson is that it pays to get in cheap (or sell high when we sell to open).

Back to the market...

Around 9am FTSE rallied again to a new high at 6307 and fell back again. But the fall was not rapid and FTSE then saw a brief move back above 6300 – this was not too encouraging for the bear case!

But this brief move to new highs is the sort of action that can stop out traders who are using spread bets to place trades and is one very solid reason why I much prefer binary bets.

For the next few hours not a great deal happened as FTSE bounced between 6310 and 6270 – in fact it looked as if we might be seeing some sort of correction before we went higher. However the failed break above 6300 remained a solid sell signal and this was still in place so I kept the faith.

While this was a happening I was fairly busy working on a new DVD series and preparing some trading examples for that series and a major seminar I was giving shortly. I find it so much easier to do this creative work when I am away from my UK office – free of many distractions. I also think my frequent visits to the beach help – there is nothing quite as inspirational as waves gently lapping a tropical shore.

The sunset was stunning as well!

FTSE starts to move

It was after midday (7pm in Phuket) that FTSE started to move. By this point I was fully positioned and prefer to leave my trades to their own devices at this point. My girlfriend was after a book of Thai fauna and flora and I had been dispatched to find it along with some solid gold earrings – hope those trades help fund them!

All through my trading career I have always tended to take profits too early – not much too early but still leaving plenty on the table. I know many traders have this problem and many never get beyond the phase where their trading results are merely a long stream of small wins and small losses.

On entries and exits

Partly this is a result of an age-old problem facing traders who choose to spread bet or trade futures – the problem of mastering two very different skills. In fact I would say they were opposing skills:

- *cutting losses* is active and disciplined,
- *running profits* is relaxed and passive.

Yet traders must learn to do them both concurrently. Not surprisingly, many fail.

This is one of the principle reasons I now use binary bets fairly exclusively. You do not need to cut losses, it is all in the price if you trade carefully, and you are free to concentrate on running those all-important profits.

This is particularly true if you trade at low prices. If you buy a binary at 10 the downside risk is strictly limited and the spread takes care of a good chunk of your risk straight off. But you have 90 points to run all the way to 100.

Anyone who has been trading for a while will know that it is not the entry that makes a trader – it is the exit. It is all too easy to make a fuss about entry with a zillion books, software programs, and gurus galore telling us all about entry. Entry is important but exit is a lot more so.

Consider three traders...

They all enter at the same point but the first one gets out because of a small pullback which gives him a small loss. The second grabs an early (and small) profit. But the third hangs in there and bags a big profit.

You won't need me to tell you which one is the successful trader of the three, but they all entered at the same price. It would have made no difference if the third trader had got in at a worse price – he would still wipe the floor with the others as far as the bottom line is concerned.

The worrying aspect is that traders tend to repeat these behavioural patterns over and over again. Yet is the difference that large?

Yes, in terms of profits. No, in every other sense.

It is much better to develop winning habits; not losing ones.

Back to the action…

Here is a chart of the whole day's price movements.

Chart 1.2: FTSE 100 Index, 26 Nov 2007

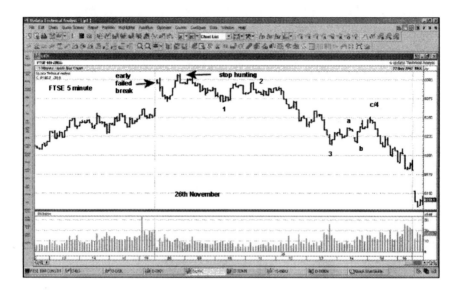

The key features are:

1. The early failed break above 6300. This sell signal was enhanced as it came in *early in the session, early in the week* and the action was quite sharp. I sold the market at this point by buying *down* binaries.

2. Despite this, FTSE decided to probe back above 6300 and, no doubt, took out a few stops in the process. The market's job is to maximise trade and when traders place stops they are showing their willingness, although not their desire, to trade. The market is happy to gobble up the business regardless.

3. Up to around midday FTSE seemed to be stuck in a range between 6270 and 6300. At that point it could have gone either way but I stuck with my positions.

4. FTSE then fell away and you can see that a five-wave form developed.

The a-b-c rally I have labelled as "4" is of note as that signalled the fifth wave decline which was essential for the profitability of my trades.

After that it was simply a matter of holding on for the ride.

Charts of the bets

I am now going to look at the charts of each bet in turn. I usually trade with IG Index which provides by far the best range of binary bets and I must thank IG for these charts which are available from their website.

FTSE to end down

I will start with the bet I passed on: *FTSE to end down*. Here is the 5-minute chart:

Chart 1.3: FTSE to end down

Although I passed (as I did not want to pay 40 for this bet) it was a clear winner and expired at 100 at the close. I know many traders are happier taking more certain profits and in this context the price of a binary bet does reflect the probability that it will be a winner. A bet at 40 can be said to have a 40% chance of success. The art of binary betting is to pick bets that cost less but still go all the way.

FTSE to end down >50

For example, I paid 11.4 for the bet *FTSE to end down >50* and I would say the odds of a decline of 50+ points were much higher than 11.4%. That is where my indicators come in. If they have any value they allow me to buy a bet at 11.4 where I think the odds are nearer 50/50.

The chart below shows the 5-minute action on this bet:

Chart 1.4: FTSE to end down >50

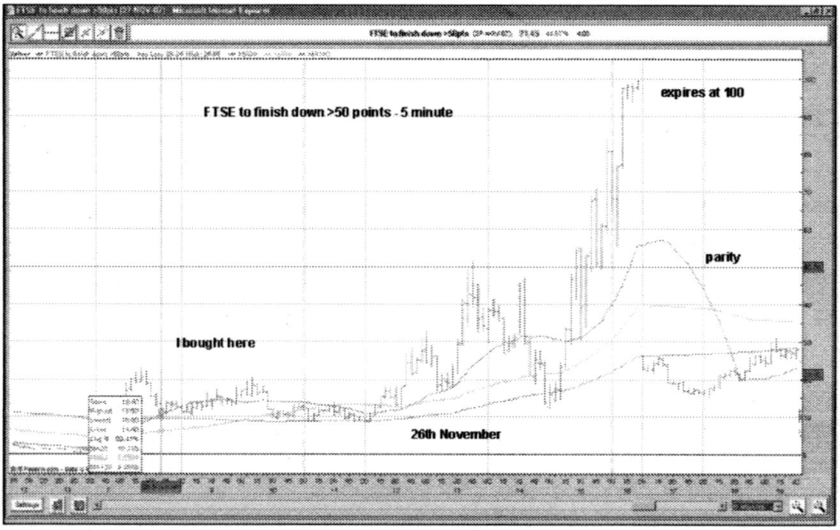

Of the three bets I am looking at this was the pick of the bunch.

Why?

Because it went all the way to 100 and it was cheap to buy! It cost 11.4 and went up to 100 offering a return of 777% on the amount at risk

In fact I generally prefer bets like *FTSE cash low to be <-100* because as soon as FTSE hits that level (i.e. sees a low more than 100 points below the prior close) the bet expires at 100 and the profit is secured. A bet *FTSE to finish…* is always less certain as whatever FTSE might do during the day, its actual close is always uncertain. For example FTSE may go 100 points down and then close 10 points up.

For this reason I am more prone to take profits on these bets at some point during the day – especially above 80 (on a bought bet). I see no point in risking 60 odd points of profit just to try and get 20 more and this is especially the case as the close looms.

FTSE cash low to be <-100

The chart below is of our final bet *FTSE cash low to be <-100* and this bet gave plenty of profit potential but did not go all the way. I bought in at 8.9 and you can see from the chart that the bet went up into the 30s just after 4pm. That is a potential return of around 200% on the risk incurred.

Chart 1.5: FTSE cash low to be <-100

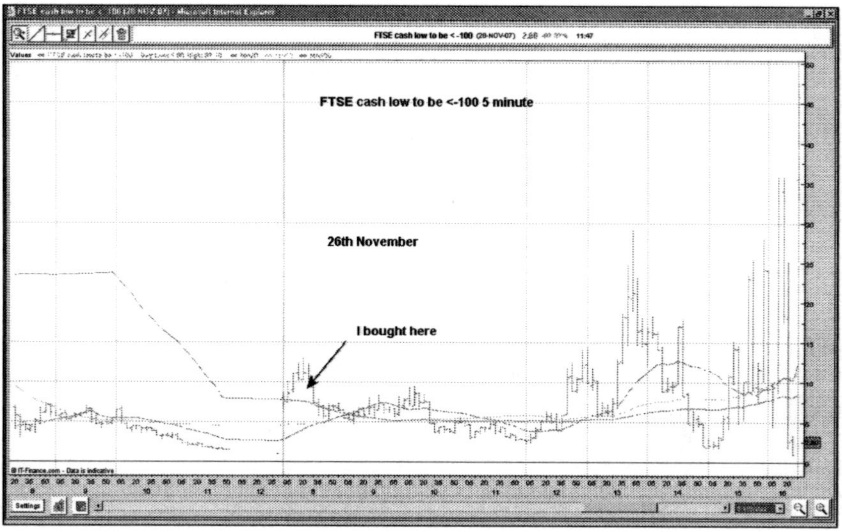

All in all a good day's trading on FTSE which illustrates quite well the way in which I approach markets. I did not get out at the best levels on either bet but the end result covered the cost of those gold earrings and I am most certainly not complaining.

> If you want to see the video clips I recorded as I made these trades please visit my website at:
> www.johnpiper.info.

Summary

In this chapter we looked at:

- Preparation before the market open
- The risk/reward on different binaries
- Adverse moves and why they are not so important
- The importance of exiting well
- Some basic chart reading
- The cost of prawns in Phuket

2.

Trading Strategies

Now that we have seen binaries in action in the real world I want to look at a few basic strategies you may wish to adopt when trading binaries. It is these strategies which will form the basis of how you trade a day like Monday 26 November 2007.

This is where we start our journey into the Aladdin's cave of binary betting!

Basic strategies

It is important to note that there are many different ways to trade binaries and it is those approaches that few other people have thought of that might prove the best.

In writing this book I see my task in two parts:

1. My primary function is to explain how binary bets and these strategies work. (Albeit I covered the basics in *Binary Betting;* my first book on this subject.)

2. But a secondary, and in some ways more important, function is to get you thinking about how you are going to use these instruments in your trading. Simply put, how you are going to make money?

So the following ideas are designed as examples which you may wish to expand upon. Ideally, come up with further ideas and add to this list.

We will look at strategies of the four following types:

1. **Buy near certainties** – If you buy at 80 and above you will most often win.

2. **Buy very cheap** – if you buy at less than 15 you have the potential to make five times your money if you get out at 90 or above.

3. **Buy low and trade the position** – perhaps for a few points a day.

4. **More complex strategies** – these may involve using binaries along with spread bets, futures and/or options.

Before I look at each of these in more detail I also want to set out a number of ways in which you can approach each of these ideas.

Different approaches to a strategy

Here are three ways in which to approach binary bets:

- **Systemise an approach** and trade it mechanically [this is covered in detail later in this book].

- **Use a set of indicators** [see below] to produce signals and then look to see which binaries may offer the best risk/reward at that time, based on what is known of the system producing the signal.

- **Approach these markets opportunistically**. Look to see what may happen and trade the binaries accordingly.

I mention *indicators* in the second point above and this term may be unfamiliar to you. There are many ways of deciding what to trade, when to do so and at what price. One of these ways is known as *technical analysis*. This involves using mathematical formulae to produce such indicators as: moving averages, stochastics and overbought/oversold. These work on a statistical basis and are designed to give traders an edge. Other traders use charts and chart patterns, and this is my own preferred way of deciding how to take positions. Yet others use fundamental analysis. All these forms of analysis – in fact any manner of taking the decision of what to trade – is valid, dependant on only one factor: *are you making money or not?*

Now we will look at the four types of strategy.

1. Buying near certainties

The price of a binary bet may be said to reflect the odds that the event will occur. For example, if we see that FTSE is up and the bet that it will close up is priced at 80/85 we might decide that the odds that it will close up are between 80% and 85%. We might take the midpoint and say the odds are 82.5%.

If this statement is correct then we do not obtain any value by trading this bet. I will show one of the reasons why it is so important.

If the binary is priced around 80 the actual spread may be 78/82.

If we assume that the odds of the event occurring are 80% that means that the event will occur on 4 out of 5 occurrences. So, if you buy the bet you will win 4 times out of 5.

Is this good?

Unfortunately it is not good enough. Here is how it works out.

Every time you buy the bet it costs you 82. You must not forget that spread! You bet at £10 per point so your stake is £820.

You win four times (meaning the bet goes to 100), and each time you win 18 points (100 – 82) at £10.

Your winnings total 4 x £180 = £720

But you lose once and you lose your entire stake of £820.

Overall Loss: £100 (£820 – £720 = £100)

So how do we turn this unfortunate result to our favour?

Here are a number of ways I have found that work:

- **Use risk control**

  If the bet goes below 50 get out. This cuts the losing bet from £820 to around £320. Be aware, however that this approach will also cull some of your winning bets – there are no free lunches!

- **Find bets that may be priced around 80 but give better odds**

  This requires a betting idea and research [discussed later in this chapter]. It is impossible for me to set out bets that will give you this advantage because if I were to include the ideas I have researched they would immediately lose their value. Others would do the same trades and this would shift the price. A small shift is enough to destroy any edge the idea had. By the time you read of the bet it would have become useless.

- **Use additional techniques to choose your trades**

  These may include fundamentals, technical indicators or chart patterns. Some traders do very well on gut instinct alone, although this can take some time to develop.

- **Find bets that complement one another**

  If one bet does go wrong the other profits. This can enhance your chances overall.

19

Later in this chapter I talk about getting "good value" from your bets and the points I make above are some of the ways in which this can be done.

2. Buying very cheap

I believe that we all have a natural tendency towards a certain style of trading or betting. It is part of our character and we are much happier if we act in accordance with our instincts and emotions. Personally, I prefer to buy cheap and my style is to do everything I can to enhance my chances of success.

Buying cheap also incorporates selling at a *high* price. I showed in *Binary Betting* how buying a binary at 30 is the same as selling one at 70 as far as potential risk and reward are concerned.

In both cases we risk 30 points and our potential reward is 70 points. In terms of risk and reward they are the same animal. The same is true if we buy at 15 or sell at 85.

But the point I made above with regard to buying high probability bets holds true. If we bet at 15 and the odds hold true we will lose. The spread will take us out. Here is how:

The true cost of the spread

If we buy at 15 the odds of success are against us and if those odds are born out we will only win one time out of every eight times. To calculate that I have assumed the spread at 10/15 and taken the mid-point which is 12.5. At 12.5 we risk that amount with a potential gain of 87.5 (100 – 12.5). That is exactly equal to odds of 8 to 1.

So we lose seven times at £10 per point.

Losses 7 x £150 (15 x £10) = £1050

We win once and make 85 points (100 – 15) = £850

Clearly this will not do

We are down £200 and the reason is the spread. But even without the spread we would still only break even. The reason for this is that betting in this way does not offer *good value*.

To work out the cost of the spread you take the cost of each bet (15) and deduct from that the cost needed to reflect the probability of 8 to 1 – that price is 12.5. So every time you trade the cost of the spread is 2.5 (15 less 12.5). Note that this is half of the actual spread of 5 points (15 less 10). We do each trade at £10 per point so each trade costs us £25 in terms of the spread. Eight trades at £25 for each one equals £200, which is our overall loss on the exercise.

How to win from cheap bets

With cheap bets it is difficult to use risk control as there is little risk to start with. But there are these options:

- Use a strategy of taking profits once you have, say, 20 points in hand. This will significantly enhance your chances of winning on any one day.

- There are also bets available which may be priced at 15 but which offer better odds. I discussed this in the section above and the same points apply to cheaper bets.

- You can also use other techniques to choose your trades again enhancing the odds. Careful selection is a key feature to profitable trading.

- There is again the option of choosing bets that complement each other.

- Cheap bets may be the best way to trade off indicators/chart patterns as these types of analysis will have a reliability quotient and as long as this quotient is better than the odds offered by the bet you will end up a winner.

3. Buy low and trade the position

We have touched on this under cheap bets when I suggested taking out a few points profit. However if we are going to trade the position we do not need to buy quite so cheaply as we will be quicker to get out.

Look again at how binary bet prices move as set out at the start of Chapter 6 of *Binary Betting*. I made the point that action between 35 and 65 can be jet-propelled. But below 20 and above 80 it gets much slower.

Why not turn that to your advantage?

21

Buy between 30 and 40, then look to exit above 60. Or sell between 60 and 70, then look to exit below 40.

Entering at those prices gives you the possibility of very quick profits but if price moves against you it would be a relatively sluggish process. It might still be fast, ultimately that depends on action in the underlying market, but profits should come in faster.

If the bet does go awry you should have plenty of time to get out at your chosen level. Maybe you only want to risk 15 points, or 20, and you simply close out if the appropriate level is hit.

With an approach like this you will need to consider your strategy carefully and here are some guidelines:

- You should ensure that your average profit equals at least two or three times your average loss.

- You must ensure that you profit at least half the time.

- If we were talking about spread betting I would add that you must not let losses run away – but that is one of the great benefits of binary bets – losses can't run away!

To end this section I will outline one critical element of system design. If you go for smaller profits there will be more of them and this is important as most traders have difficulty with lots of losses and a few profits. We all like making money most days if possible. But clearly the important thing is to come out on top overall and these two goals sometimes prove mutually incompatible.

4. More complex strategies

Here are a few ideas which you may find useful:

- The Tunnels and the OneTouches might be used as an unusual *stop*. With FTSE at +/- 15 a 55/55 Tunnel may be priced at 70/75 depending on volatility and time. Buying a future/spread betting away from the Tunnel and selling the Tunnel might be useful. If the Tunnel is touched you keep your 70, if the future benefits you make money on that. This could be combined with an in-the-money up/down bet.

- Sometimes it may make sense to buy longer dated up/down bets (i.e. daily) and sell shorter dated ones (i.e. hourly).

- You will sometimes find that different betting sites offer arbitrage opportunities as touched on in Chapter 5 of *Binary Betting*.

- If you buy a OneTouch and sell another at a different level you will achieve profit/losses at different levels. For example, if FTSE is at 6000 you might buy the 6040 OneTouch at 50 (bet #1), then sell the 6060 at 15 (bet #2). As these are OneTouches it is the high of the day that is important and the close or low is irrelevant. Here is how these bets would work out:

- If FTSE's high is below 6040 you lose a net 35 points (50 down on bet #1 and 15 up on bet #2).

- If FTSE's high is above 6040 but below 6060 you make 65 points (50 up on bet #1 and 15 up on bet #2).

- If FTSE's high is above 6060 you lose a net 35 points (50 up on bet #1 and 85 down on bet #2).

- If you enter the bets in the example above at different times then you may get better prices but this is not guaranteed.

- You can also put in place similar structures with Tunnels and/or other bets.

I have kept this section fairly short and sweet as more complex structures are something of an acquired taste and those so inclined will want to do the research themselves. The ideas above may provide a useful starting point.

Having looked at four different groups of strategies, we'll now turn to research.

Research

It is important to research betting ideas to give yourself better odds of success.

As an example I will look at a fairly high priced bet which would be expected to come good. I include the Dow 100/100 Tunnel in this category. This bet goes to 100 if the Dow stays in a range 100 points either side of the prior close. It goes to zero if the Dow touches those extremes.

But how often does it do this?

This is a good example of something you can test for yourself. Get hold of daily data on the Dow going back a year and work out how often the Dow will stay in this Tunnel. You will find it is well above half the time.

What is the price of the bet?

It will vary from day to day but what price would you find attractive? Once you know that, all you need to do is monitor the market and then take the price when it becomes available.

Conversely, the 60/60 Tunnel on the Dow will be taken out far more often and if you trade these instruments you need to be aware of the statistics. If you know that the Dow or FTSE has a less than 25% chance of exceeding a range and you have bought a Tunnel with that range it will make far more sense to hold to expiry as the Tunnel will close at 100 if the market does stay within the range. But if the odds are nearer 70% that would be an entirely different matter.

(I have given partial answers to some of the questions raised by the above in the Appendix. There is also more information in Chapter 10.)

It is important to check out such data yourself as this could be the foundation stone of your trading system. If you are going to become an expert in your system you need to put in the groundwork.

> One of the reasons why so many fail at trading is that they simply do not do the background work. You need to decide on your style of betting/trading and then research every aspect exhaustively.

In Chapter 6 of *Binary Betting* I gave as an example a high bet on the Dow. Here too some simple research can give you extremely valuable information. How often will the Dow close in a range between 60 and 80? It is not difficult to find out and once you know you can judge whether this bet gives you an edge.

Pricing and probability

The pricing of a sports bet

With a sports bet all the time the game is played, or the race is run, the binary bet prices will be changing giving you more opportunities.

With a football game the price will reflect the probability of either side winning the game, some of the key factors being:

1. the number of goals scored and by who,

2. the time remaining, and

3. whether any men have been sent off.

The concept of value

But it is important to note that although the price will reflect the probability; it will not be *the* probability. Other factors will influence price, for example how much money is on each team.

My statement:

> *the price will reflect the probability; it will not be the probability*

may confuse you but it is an essential point. There is a concept known as *value* which is often applied to bets generally. Professional gamblers are very familiar with the concept as it is how and why they win. A bet has value if it offers better odds than the event itself would lead you to expect. So if the horse, Mr. Splodge, with a binary priced at 8/11, has a 25% chance of winning the binary price should really be 23/27 or thereabouts.

If you can buy a bet which should be priced at 23/27 at 8/11 then you are clearly getting good value. Similarly if the bet is priced at 8/11 and there really is a 25% chance of Mr. Splodge winning the race then the price of 8/11 may be an attempt to reflect the probability of the event but it will clearly not be that probability – which is 25%.

It was this concept I was referring to when I was talking earlier about the art of binary betting and said that you should

> *give yourself a further edge by choosing bets with a higher probability of success.*

Don't be concerned if you have trouble with this at this stage. This is something you will develop a feel for as you become more experienced.

The pricing of a financial bet

If you are betting on a financial market, perhaps the FTSE 100 Index, then throughout the session the binary prices will be moving to reflect three factors:

1. The time left on the bet until expiry.

2. The price of the underlying market as distinct from the price of the bet itself. In particular how far up or down the market is on the day.

3. Volatility – the speed of market action.

How far up or down a market moves is a measure of its distance from *parity* and I define parity as when the market (or index) is unchanged over the relevant period. This period may be a day or a week or an hour, among other time frames. Many binary bets are based on the prior close and in that case it is how far the market is up or down since that prior close that is important. But if we are looking at an hourly bet which may run from 3pm to 4pm then it is the "close" at 3pm that is important.

However, *weight of money* is also an important factor and prices will move as money flows in one particular direction. One of the betting companies told me they work on the assumption that if a lot of money goes onto a bet they have mis-priced it.

> Some would see this as manipulation or as unfair. But a successful trader will see it as an opportunity!

A final word on pricing

I have said that binary bets can only move between 0 and 100. In fact, although almost every bet I have ever seen has been priced between 0 – 100 there is no reason why other prices may not be chosen, say 32 – 212 (a Fahrenheit scale), or -50 – +50 (where parity is zero). But 0 – 100 is far easier to understand.

I have seen some bets priced differently, as I said in *Binary Betting*. For example, on TV's X-Factor where the pricing was that the winner's binary rose to 50, the 2nd place to 30, 3rd to 20 and 4th to 10. Together these add up to 100. This can also be the case with horse racing and is why the brief example I gave above on Mr. Splodge may be quoted differently in the real world.

I am told that the very early binaries were priced between 1 and 10 but this is no longer the case.

Summary

In this chapter we looked at four strategies:

1. Buying near certainties – high probability bets

2. Buying very cheap bets

3. Buying low and the trading the bet

4. More complex strategies

We then looked at the key factors that affect binary prices and discussed the probability of success.

3.

The Key Bets

In this chapter we are going to look in detail at the principal bets, offer suggestions for how you might like to use them and back this up with examples.

We are now going to look at five of the more interesting binaries for an in-depth analysis of what you can do with them. The five bets are:

1. Up/Down (reversals)
2. Tunnels/Barrier Bets
3. OneTouches
4. Hi/Los
5. Football Match – play for the goal

Up/Down (reversals)

In fact there is no bet for a market to *reverse* but this is how I classify the Up/Down bets. For example, if I bet on *FTSE to close up* or *FTSE to close down* I generally buy them when they are less than 50. So I will buy the *FTSE to close down* when FTSE is up and the *FTSE to close up* when FTSE is down. If I am to win, FTSE must reverse.

I must stress that this is just the way I trade and it does not mean you should do the same thing. You will have more successful trades if you buy *FTSE to close up* when FTSE is up. But you will pay more for the bet and your profits will be less – it is your decision as to which is the best way to trade these instruments.

To repeat a basic point: the bet will go to 100 if the event occurs, i.e. if FTSE does close up/down, and go to zero if the event does not occur.

Here are three ways in which to profit from this form of bet:

1. Small moves

A small move by the underlying market can have a substantial effect on the binary price – especially if that small move takes the underlying from up to down, or vice versa. Another way of saying this is that the small move takes the underlying market through parity.

For example, if FTSE is 5 points up and it is 2pm then the *FTSE to end up* bet may be priced at around 55/60 reflecting the fact that the market has two and a half hours before it closes.

At the same time the *FTSE to end down* bet would be priced at 40/45 – remember that the bets are a mirror image of each other, both sides adding up to 100.

If FTSE now moves 12 points down and takes an hour doing it then the price of *FTSE to end down* may now be 66/70 reflecting the fact that FTSE is now down 7 points and there is only an hour and a half until it closes.

Here is how you might trade this:

Table 3.1: Small move trade

Time and action	Price of *FTSE to end down*
2pm FTSE is up 5 points	40/45
Buy at 45	
Risk control – plan to exit if price drops to 20	
3pm FTSE is down 7 points	66/70
Sell at 66 – **profit** 21 points (66 less 45)	
Cash profit at £10 per point – £210 (21 x £10)	

2. Extremes

Traders often look to catch highs or lows and these sometimes occur in fast market conditions. This poses problems for spread betters because risk is enhanced. If the spread better wants to risk a maximum of 20 points he has a problem because:

- In fast markets 20 points may take around 20 seconds

- He can never be sure where the high or low comes in

In the table below I set out how a spread better and a binary better may do in such a situation.

Table 3.2: Trading an extreme

Market Action	Spread Better	Binary Better
FTSE opens down 40 points at 6120	Buys FTSE at 6122 (spread 6118/6122) for £10 per point	Buys FTSE to end up at 6 (bet priced at 3/6) at £10 per point, risking £60
Risk control	Places stop at 6102 (risking 20 points) – maximum exposure huge	None – maximum exposure 6 points/£60
FTSE rallies 20 points to 6140	Spread goes to 6138/6142 – holds	Bet now priced at 12/15 – holds
FTSE falls 50 points to 6090	Stopped out – loss 20 points – at £10 per point cash loss £200	Bet now priced at 0/3 – buys at 3 at £20 per point risking a further £60
FTSE rallies 30 points to 6120 – same as opening level	Thinks this may be the low and waits for a pullback to enter again	Bet now priced at 3/6 – holds
FTSE rallies 20 points to 6140	Now absolutely sure the low is in. Buys FTSE at 6142 (spread 6138/6142) for £10 per point	Bet now priced at 8/12 – holds
Risk control	Places stop at 6122 (risking 20 points) – maximum exposure huge	None – maximum exposure £120
FTSE falls 30 points to 6110	Stopped out – loss 20 points – at £10 per point cash loss £200. **Total Loss now £400 and no open positions**	Bet again priced at 0/3 – considers buying more but feels exposure is sufficient. **Paper loss is now £120 but is still positioned**
FTSE rallies 40 points to 6150 and now only down 10 on the prior close. It is now 2.45pm (GMT) and the Dow has opened up	Now incredibly frustrated and hand hurts from thumping desk	Bet now priced at 30/34 – sells at 30 for £10 per point, brings in £300. Total position cost £120 so £180 up and remaining positions for free
FTSE rallied another 20 points and is now at 6170 up 10 on the day, Dow up 50, it is now 3:30pm (GMT) with one our to go	Opens the first of a number of beers	Bet now priced at 66/70 – sells at 66 for £10 per point, brings in £660 clear profit and remaining positions for free
FTSE closes at 6182, up 22 on the day	Has gone to the pub, could no longer bear to watch the action, thinks hand may be broken!	Bet closes at 100 – at £10 per point that brings in a further £1000 clear profit and remaining positions for free
Closing position	**Total loss £400** (despite being right when sure low was in) and bad hangover and was right again – hand is broken! Approaches next day's trading with fear and trepidation	**Profit of £1840** (total sales £1960, less cost £120) – feels great the following day and trades with confidence

I know many spread betters who would relate to the spread better's side of this story and I have been there myself. Although I have never actually broken my hand, I have had the hangovers.

The key point here is that the binary better can relax because he is never exposed beyond the cost of the bets. So he is not subject to the – sometimes extreme – emotions which can be triggered when market action goes against us. To make money in this situation the market would need to rally strongly and this will not always be the case, but those using binaries can stay positioned whatever the market throws at them and can then take the rewards that may be offered.

3. Very low risk

This is an example of a bet I placed myself in the first few days of 2007. US markets had put in a good performance in the first hour or so on Wednesday, 4 January 2007, its first trading session of the New Year, and the Dow was up around 120 points. That rally had traced out five waves which is one of the trading techniques I use when looking for possible reversals and those five waves gave me a sell signal.

When that sell signal was given I was able to buy the bet *Wall Street to end down* for 3.9. Now, as you now know, binaries can only move between zero and 100. Buying at 3.9 means that my total risk was 3.9 points and at £10 per point my risk was £39. But my potential reward was 96.1 (100 – 3.9) which comes in at over 24 times my risk. There is no other trading vehicle which offers anything close to that sort of risk/reward ratio, certainly not futures, options nor spread betting.

In the event US markets plunged down and the bet went above 90. To put this in monetary terms at £10 per point your total risk would have been £39 – potential reward £900!

That is what I like about binaries.

Tunnels/Barrier Bets

With a Tunnel or barrier bet it is critical to read the bet description carefully. Some go to 100 when the underlying market stays within the designated range. For example, the FTSE +50/-50 Tunnel will go to 100 if FTSE does not make a high or a low 50 points or more away from the prior close. Others go to 100 if the range is broken. Some are even more complex and only go to 100 if the underlying market penetrates both extremes.

Here are two ways in which to profit from this form of bet.

1. Support levels

There are three main classifications of market action. The market can either:

1. go up

2. go down, or

3. go sideways

There are times when it is likely that the market will do something but we do not know what. For example, if a market comes down to a level from which it has previously rallied strongly (such a level is known as *support*) a number of traders will be looking for another strong rally. But these traders know that if support breaks the market may fall sharply.

In such a situation the obvious trade may be to buy the market at support. This could be done as in the example set out in the following table (Table 3.3) and if we get the direction right that is fine.

But what if support breaks?

In the table we contrast the behaviour of a Tunnel with a more conventional *up* bet.

For the remainder of this section I am going to refer to these bets as Tunnels and they will go to 100 if the underlying market stays within the designated range.

Table 3.3: Trading at support level

Market Action	Binary Tunnel Bet	Binary Up Bet
FTSE opens down 15 points at 6000 – a key support level	FTSE +55/-55 Tunnel priced at 45/50 – trader thinks a bounce from 6000 is likely which will raise the Tunnel price and as he expects strong action he is looking to sell the Tunnel – so he waits	Buys FTSE to end up at 36 (bet priced at 33/36) at £10 per point, risking £360. As FTSE is not down significantly the bet is more expensive
Risk Control	None – no position	None at this point – maximum exposure 36 points/£360
FTSE rallies 20 points to 6020 now up 5 points – it is now midday	FTSE +55/-55 Tunnel now priced at 70/75 – trader sells at 70 at £10 per point. Maximum risk £300 (100 less 70 x £10)	Bet now priced at 55/60 – trader unhappy with fairly weak rally and closed half the position at 55. Cash in £275 (55 at £5 per point)
FTSE falls 61 points to 5959	FTSE +55/-55 Tunnel goes to zero as FTSE has gone outside the range. **Cash Profit £700**	Bet now priced at 0/3 – no action can be taken on existing position and trader is not inclined to buy at 3 as market is below support
FTSE closes at 5971 down 44 points	The close has no effect as the bet has already expired	Bet closes at zero. **Overall Loss £85** (cost of £360 less sale at £275)

In this example we may consider both traders to be fortunate as the market rallied off the early low which gave the Tunnel trader the opportunity to sell at a better price and the *FTSE to end up* trader the chance to profit on half of his position and limit his eventual loss. But, on the other hand, markets do tend to bounce at support – which is why it is called *support* in the first place! It is simply that such bounces do not always last for long.

2. Longer-term moves

Most of the bets we have looked at have been short term, most daily, but some of a shorter duration. But there are longer-term bets, not just the weekly up/downs, but some lasting up to six months.

(For these we must visit www.BetOnMarkets.com and www.BetsForTraders.com.)

Here is an example:

The market you follow, FTSE in this case, has been going sideways for some months and the chart action has formed a triangular formation. This is a fairly well known chart pattern and the chart below shows the action.

Chart 3.1: FTSE triangulates (1)

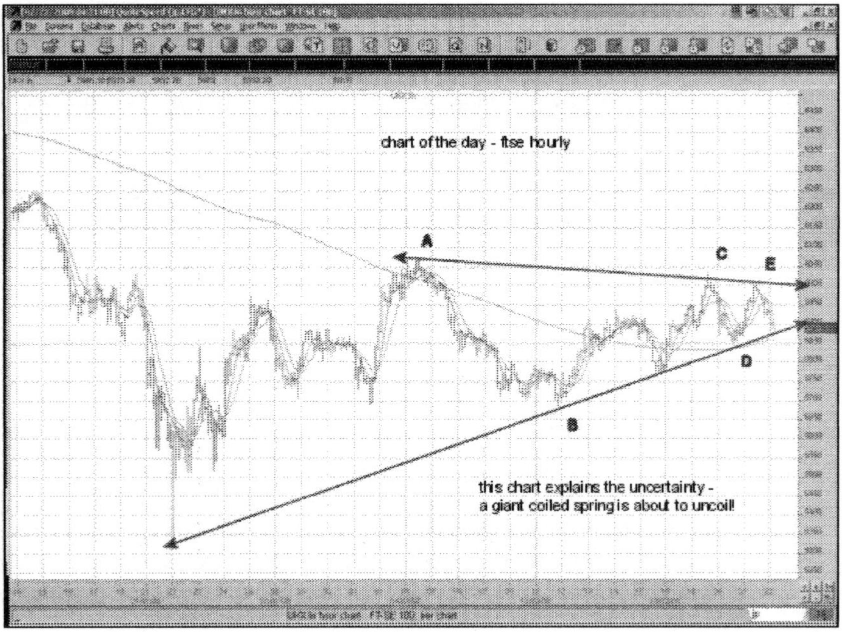

You will see that I have labelled the waves of the triangle A, B, C, D, and E on the chart above and triangles are generally formed of five waves. Also you will notice that the triangle stays pretty closely within the two trendlines I have drawn on the chart. Finally you will see from the chart below the triangle was followed by a false break to the upside and then the true break came to the downside.

Chart 3.2: FTSE triangulates (2)

Triangles are like coiled springs. The market moves in a tighter and tighter range and everyone expects a breakout but no one is sure in which direction. Our binary trader knows two things at this point:

1. That a breakout will come

2. That it has the potential to be a significant move

With these two factors in mind the trader will consider the action on the market he is watching and in particular look at:

- The length of time that the triangle has lasted. In the chart above FTSE was triangulating for around 5 weeks. This is a fairly short-term triangle.

- The maximum width of the triangle; as this provides a guide for subsequent action. In the chart the maximum width is about 800 points.

With these points in mind the trader decides once he can count fives waves for the triangle on FTSE that he will sell a 300 point Tunnel with an expiry approximately 5 weeks from here. The first chart above shows this and he logs onto www.BetOnMarkets.com and this bet is called an *up and down* and is listed under the heading *boundaries*. Alternatively he may go to www.BetsForTraders.com where the bet is called a *one-touch range*.

This bet will go to 100 if either boundary is touched. Our trader enters his chosen criteria in the relevant boxes and finds he is offered very low odds on this bet; in binary terms he has to pay around 90 for this trade which he considers far too high. In fact this is not unreasonable – a lot can happen in 5 weeks – in fact if you look at Chart 3.2 above you can see that the bet would have been an outright winner 3 or 4 weeks later.

One other factor which I might usefully mention at this point is that as the triangle continues to develop this will reduce *volatility* in the market. Volatility is a measure of how much is happening. If not much is happening volatility is said to be low and this is one of the factors that does affect binary prices. The *up and down* or *one-touch range* bets we are looking at here should be cheaper in a time of low volatility than at a time of high volatility.

Our trader decides to wait until he sees a breakout above or below the triangle trendlines. By doing so he can reduce the time frame and this will give him a much better price.

The breakout comes, see Chart 3.2 above, and he prices the same 300 point Tunnel but with an expiry only 3 weeks from now. He is now asked to pay 62 for this bet with an expectation of a 38 point profit if the market moves 300 points over the coming month. He bets at £10 per point so risks £620 to make a potential £380. He can also exit early either to reduce his risk exposure or to take profits.

2 weeks later he wins his bet – even though the initial breakout was a false break to the upside!

You will notice that he has chosen a 300 point move which is somewhat less than the maximum width of the triangle. He wanted a time frame equivalent to that of the triangle itself but had to settle for less to get the price he wanted.

As I wrote this the move was still in progress, but check the chart of FTSE for yourself to see the full move that came in from this signal – as we go to press late in 2008 it is still going!

OneTouches

In one respect the OneTouch is half of a Tunnel bet. As I have said, a Tunnel is useful when we are not sure of market direction. It can also be useful when we may feel sure of market direction but get it wrong. In this context it can make sense to trade a Tunnel even if you are sure. But there are times when a Tunnel bet is either not available or is too expensive.

Here is one way in which to profit from this form of bet in such a situation:

Using a OneTouch after an early fall

Table 3.4: Trading a OneTouch

Market Action	Binary Tunnel Bet	Binary OneTouch Bet
FTSE opens down 40 points at 6102	*FTSE +35/-35 Tunnel* immediately goes to zero and ceases to be available	We expect the market to reverse and prefer the OneTouch as it will go to 100 if touched, whereas a *FTSE to close up* bet would only go to 100 if FTSE is up at the close. We buy the 6150 OneTouch at 16 for £10 per point
Risk Control	None – no position	None at this point – maximum exposure £160 (16 at £10 per point)
Midday: FTSE rallies 20 points to 6122 now down 20 points	As FTSE is now nearer parity the Tunnel bets are now more expensive making them more attractive to sell. The +50/-50 Tunnel is now priced at 78/82 but our OneTouch offers better risk/reward	Bet now priced at 27/32 – no action at this point
FTSE falls 10 points to 6112	No change to Tunnel prices as move away from parity counter balanced by time decay	Bet now priced at 12/15 – no action
3:30pm: FTSE rallies 35 points to 6147, now up 5	Tunnel prices now very high as FTSE near parity with close only an hour away but too late for a sharp move to be likely	Bet now priced at 87/92 as only 3 points away from being touched. We close half position at 87 for a profit of 71 points (87 less 16). At £5 per point our profit is £355
4pm: FTSE falls 15 points to 6132, now down 10 points	No change	Bet now priced at 22/25 and illustrates how a fairly small move can have a big effect especially as expiry nears. We grind our teeth.
FTSE closes at 6135, down 7 points		The remaining bet expires at zero for a loss of 16 points. At £5 per point this amounts to £80. **Our net profit is £275** – the profit of £355 less the loss of £80.

Hi/Los

As set out in Chapter 5 of *Binary Betting* these bets allow us to bet on where the high and/or low will fall during the day.

Here are two ways in which to profit from this form of bet:

1. Extremes

Hi/Los provide another way of playing extremes. Maybe you believe a key high or low is in but are not convinced that sharp action is going to follow immediately. In this situation an up/down bet may not yield any profit but the Hi/Lo will do well.

Table 3.5: Trading an extreme with a Hi/Lo bet

Market Action	Binary Hi/Lo Bet	Binary Up Bet
FTSE opens down 40 points at 6120	No action at this point – we want to see some evidence that a low is in	Buys *FTSE to end up* at 6 (bet priced at 3/6) at £10 per point, risking £60
Risk Control	None – no position in place	None – maximum exposure 6 points/£60
FTSE rallies 20 points to 6140	We now look for the market to re-test the low to confirm it is important	Bet now priced at 12/15 – holds
FTSE falls 51 points to 6089 down 71 points	We now have far more extreme action and we are looking for a low	Bet now priced at 0/3 – buys at 3 at £20 per point risking a further £60
FTSE rallies 31 points to 6120 – same as opening level	During this rally the bet *low to be down between 70 and 80 points* now priced at 34/40 and we buy at 40 at £10 per point	Bet now priced at 3/6 – holds
FTSE rallies 20 points to 6140	Bet now priced at 72/75 – note how much better we are doing already as it is now very likely that the low is in, whereas FTSE still has a long way to go before it is up on the day	Bet now priced at 8/12 – holds
Risk Control	Sell at 72 at £3 per point. Bringing in £216 (73 at £3) and this reduces total risk to £184 (£400 less £216)	None – maximum exposure £120
FTSE falls 30 points to 6110	Bet now priced at 65/70 – time is moving on and it remains highly likely that the low is in so this move has little effect on the price of the bet	Bet again priced at 0/3 – considers buying more but feels exposure is sufficient. **Paper loss is now £120 but is still positioned**
FTSE rallies 10 points to 6120 and is now down 40 on the prior close. It is now 2.45pm (GMT) and the Dow has opened flat	Bet now priced at 82/87	Bet still priced at 0/3 – nothing to be done
FTSE closes at 6132, down 28 on the day	Bet closes at 100 and at £10 per point this brings in a further £700 (100 at £7)	Bet closes at zero
Closing Position	Total Profit £516 – cash received of £916 (£216 plus £700) less original cost at £400 (40 at £10 per point)	Loss of £120

2. Trending action

It is something of a truism that when we look at a chart of market action some of us see the highs and the lows (what I also refer to as the extremes) and some of us see the moves between the highs and the lows – and these moves are called *trends*.

Similarly some traders look to make money out of the highs and lows and others like to profit from the trends. The Hi/Lo bet is one way of doing both. I set out above how this bet can be useful with an extreme low and I now use a very similar example to show how it can be used when a market is trending – meaning the trader expects the market to continue in the same direction and not make a key high or low.

Table 3.6: Trading the trend with a Hi/Lo bet

Market and Trading Action	Binary Hi/Lo Bet
FTSE opens down 45 points at 6115	No action at this point as we are looking to sell a Lo bet and they are quite cheap at this point as no low has been established.
Risk control	None – no position in place.
FTSE rallies 20 points to 6135	During this rally the bet *low to be down between 40 and 50 points* becomes priced at 40/45 and we sell at 40 at £10 per point.
FTSE falls 50 points to 6085 down 75 points	The low can no longer be between 40 and 50 points down and so our bet goes to zero. We pocket £400 (40 points at £10 per point) We wait for further opportunities…
FTSE rallies 35 points to 6120 – same as opening level	At the end of this rally the bet *low to be down between 70 and 80 points* is priced at 64/70 and we sell at 64 at £10 per point.
FTSE falls 45 points to 6075	The low can no longer be between 70 and 80 points down and so our bet goes to zero. We pocket £640 (64 points at £10 per point). We have taken a **total profit of £1040** (£400 plus £640) and call it a day.

Football Match – play for the goal

In the previous chapter I touched on the key point that binaries differ from many other forms of betting in that the bet can be traded at any time between when you open the bet and when it expires. We have looked at this from the point of view of financial bets extensively. Now we are going to look at it from the perspective of a sports fan who wants to make money from a football match.

Example 3.1: Football match

Arsenal are playing West Ham and the bet *Arsenal to win* is priced at 51/56 and the bet *West Ham to win* is priced at 29/34.[1]

You favour Arsenal but think it is over-priced. So you bet on West Ham to win (you pay 34). You go for £10 per point and your risk is £340 (34 x £10) and your potential profit is £660 (66 x £10).

The match starts and West Ham get off to a roaring start scoring the first goal after 10 minutes and Arsenal have a key man sent off. The binary price jumps to 65/68. This means that you could sell the bet at 65 – you are well up!

You decide you are going to sell, you sell at 65 and bag 31 points (the 65 sale price less you purchase price at 34) at £10 per point = Profit £310.

The match continues and Arsenal come back into the game and score two goals. Suddenly the *West Ham to win* price drops to 5/8.

It's too good to miss, you buy at 8…

The following chart shows these movements.

---

[1] These two bets do not add up to 100 because there is a third bet Arsenal and West Ham to draw priced a 10/15.

Figure 3.3: binary price chart during a football match

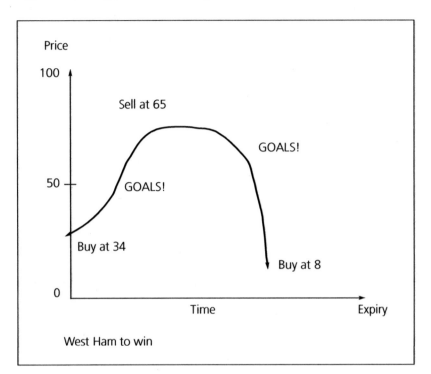

The strategy here is: bet on a lowly priced team and then get out when they score the first goal.

I was watching just such a game and a goal was scored. The binary price jumped from 20-24 to 88-92. This is extraordinary behaviour – and not something that one finds normally in financial markets.

Summary

In this chapter we have taken an in-depth look at five of the more interesting binary bets and examined a number of ways in which they can be used. The five bets are:

1. Up/Down (reversals)

2. Tunnels/Barrier Bets

3. OneTouches

4. Hi/Los

5. Football Match – play for the goal

Part II – Strategies

4.

Shorting FTSE with BetOnMarkets.com

When FTSE crashed through 5800 on Monday 21 January 2008 the bets I had recommended to my clients earlier in the month saw a very healthy profit.

To win £1000 the cost of some of these bets has been less than £100. When trading binary bets it rarely gets much better than this. Certainly I have bought a bet at 2 and seen it go all the way to 100, but that is a relatively rare event.

In fact it never gets better than that if you do not trade binary bets. If you spread bet, buy or sell options, or trade any other vehicles you will never get those sort of returns at that sort of risk. If you can buy a bet at 10 or less that is the best risk/reward I have ever seen.

Markets heading for a big fall!

In this chapter I am going to explain how I chose those bets, among others, and I am going to tell you why I thought FTSE was going to fall so fast. I recommended the bets when FTSE was around the 6200 level and that was on 11 January. I needed FTSE to fall 400 points in a little more than 2 weeks for some of these bets to win. In the event it did a lot more than that!

But this story really starts back on 11 June 2007 when I asked around 15,000 investors the question: "are markets heading for a BIG fall?" – a rhetorical question as my accompanying article concluded that they were indeed.

On 11 June there were no clouds in the sky and few people would have known a sub-prime mortgage if it had bitten them on the butt!

That call on 11 June was heavily based around the futures and options expiry on 15 June – known as the *triple witching hour*. It was just after expiry on 18 June that FTSE peaked at 6751. It then fell over 900 points (a big fall in my book) to see a low at 5821 on 17 August. I should mention that FTSE did see a bounce in July to a new high at 6754, but this was a failed break (a clear sell signal in its own right) and merely added to the negatives in place at that time.

That was the first piece of the jigsaw and the resistance established that day – around 6750 – has proven effective ever since (as I write in December 2008).

51

The importance of options expiry

But before we go on to the next piece of the jigsaw I need to explain why expiry is so important.

There are two reasons I have identified:

- Some of the really big players sell options and they will move the market as expiry nears. Some of these are sold in the process of selling them to those who want to buy options but they also sell for their own book. These players can move the market and the market tends to see sharp swings in the sessions leading up to expiry as the bigger players jockey for position. By looking at the open interest in the various option strikes on the S&P you can see where the biggest open interest lies and often expiry is fairly close to that level. If you doubt this then check it out.

- You will also find, if you do the research, that the two weeks directly before expiry tend to be calmer than the two weeks directly after expiry. (Every now and then there are five weeks between one expiry and another but that does not alter this factor.)

The action immediately after expiry can be wild. The 1987 Crash is the best example I know. But 21 January 2008 was another more recent example – the really fast action came immediately after expiry on 18 January. Options expiry is a feature I use in many of my forecasts.

Fear brings on what is feared

The major players keep the markets in a range running up to expiry because that suits their book. Afterwards they let them rip because that gives them the opportunity to sell options at high prices and this is aided by the fact that all those traders who had bought options have just seen them expire. So they buy some more – maybe as a form of portfolio insurance.

But fear brings on the object of the fear and as investors buy put options so the big traders sell futures to hedge their exposure to the put options they have sold and so the market falls back!

There is a certain amount of hypothesising in this but the fact remains that we do see the fast action immediately after expiry – that is indisputable.

It is also generally quieter before expiry.

But the major players do not have it all their own way and I suspect the market was simply too strong to contain before the expiry in January 2008 and October 2008. It is important to realise that what may happen in the general case does not happen all the time.

A case in point is the September 2008 expiry. The market was well down on the Wednesday before expiry when "good" news was suddenly announced and I believe that was accompanied by a large amount of orchestrated buying which served to push the expiry level much, much closer to the prior level in August 2008. I suspect a lot of the major players would have been crucified by an expiry at the lower levels and something had to be done – the "bailout" plan was launched!

I have spent a bit of time on this point and for a good reason. I think any trader of the major indices can only benefit from this analysis and an understanding of the effect options expiry has on the market.

Back to the price action…

A major sell signal in November 2007

The peaks in June and July 2007 were the start of the problems that the market has been dealing with ever since. But markets always bounce on their way, up and down, and we saw a very solid bounce following the low at 5821 in August. In fact FTSE managed to make it to 6751 and then fell once more. This was another sell signal; we now had quite a few in our collection, because:

1. That move was a failed re-test of the prior high at 6754

2. It established the presence of minus development above 6750[2]

---

[2] *Minus development* is a term from Market Profile. All these terms are explained in my book *The Way To Trade* – see also the Appendix of this book.

Then on 2 November I issued a major sell signal. Here is part of my commentary that day together with the accompanying chart:

> FTSE has now seen five waves down – see chart below – and I am treating this as a major sell signal. On Thursday I said we had a "clear sell signal in the form of a spike high above 6700 and a failed re-test of Monday's high at 6726." All well and good, but we now have confirmation of an impulsive decline off the top with a complete wave pattern, albeit involving a failure, into the peak.
>
> It is my view the markets are finally accepting that the global economy is between the rock and the hard place. Interest rate cuts may help with one part of the problem but currency fluctuations, among other things, simply aggravate other parts of the problem. If markets can shrug of this decline then I can only think it is a massive buy signal – but that I do *not* expect.

Chart 4.1: FTSE (November 2007)

The very fast action we have seen in 2008 stemmed from this sell signal back in November 2007 and here is how it looks on a more recent chart:

Chart 4.2: FTSE, anatomy of a fall

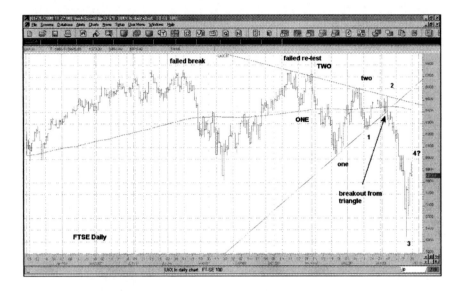

I do not want to write a book about technical analysis (although I guess I already have!) but there are a fair range of sell signals shown on this chart as follows:

1. The failed break and the later failed re-test I have already mentioned above.

2. The Elliott Wave patterns; in particular the initial five-wave decline shown on the earlier chart.

3. The breakout below the triangle – a well-documented triangle at that.

4. There were also longer-term trendlines on the weekly chart which had been broken.

Fast action

This explains why I expected FTSE to go down and I had similar expectations on other major equity indices worldwide.

But why did I expect fast action?

Because "fast" action is the key to getting fantastic returns on longer-term binary bets of the sort offered by BetOnMarkets and their competitor BetsForTraders.

For this I must explain a little about the Elliott Wave Theory. To put it simply (I am assuming those who are interested will want to follow up with research of their own), back in the 1930s Elliott identified a pattern whereby impulsive moves were formed of five waves as set out in this illustration.

Figure 4.1: Elliot's five waves

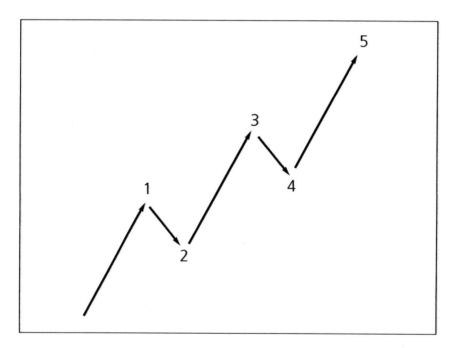

He also discovered that the third wave was usually the longest and the fastest. My experience is exactly that; when we get to a "third of a third" it can be explosive!

The decline I recommended shorting on 11 January was more than just a "third of a third" it was a "third of a third of a third". If you look again at the daily chart ("anatomy of a fall") you can see that it formed a part of THREE, a part of three and is labelled 3 itself. So the wave itself was "3" – the third part of "three" – which itself was the third part of "THREE". This may seem confusing but Elliott Waves are *fractal* and a later chapter looks at Elliott Waves in more detail.

Plus don't forget that we also had options expiry on 18 January.

The scene was most definitely set.

Dark forces and a 1000 point fall

I will quickly add one final piece of the jigsaw: this was the rather feeble performance over the Christmas period. This led me to inform the fortunate 15,000 on 16 December 2007 that there were "dark forces gathering." I had also mentioned that I expected a fall in excess of 1000 points – in the event from top to bottom FTSE fell 1416 points.

But what is more important, and what I am trying to do here, is to give you a feel for how to use these various techniques in the real world.

Now we are going to turn to another key issue…

Choosing the bets

It is one thing identifying trading opportunities and although I mention the "p" word above it is not really about prediction. Traders do not predict, they search out opportunities whereby they obtain an edge. The edge may be small but over a number of trades it will make itself felt and result in overall and consistent profitability over time.

For example, many traders may have a hit rate of less than 50% and this would give the lie to any claims of predictive ability. But when they win, they may average a profit double their average on losing trades.

Assuming such profits and losses include all costs (such as commissions where applicable) then as long as one in three trades are winners the trader will break even. If he wins 40% of the time then that is an edge he can take to the bank.

One important point is: although I was pretty certain markets were due to fall a more tricky question was when!

But when I recommended those bets on 11 January 2008 I had three factors in my favour:

1. Expiry was coming up

2. The Elliott pattern was suggesting "third of a third" type action

3. The Xmas rally had been disappointing suggesting "dark forces" were about to be unleashed.

At the start of this article I mentioned the 5800 level. Some of the bets I was talking about were the 5800 OneTouches. If you buy a OneTouch it will be an outright winner if the specified level is touched. But there are other ways to play a possible decline than merely buying a OneTouch and I did recommend other bets as set out below.

The bets themselves

Here is a complete list of the bets I recommended at the time–

1. On 9 January 2008 to buy the 6408 NoTouch with BetOnMarkets expiring on 8 April 2008 – guide price £22 per £100 of possible winnings

2. On 9 January 2008 to buy the 6430 NoTouch with BetsForTraders expiring on 18 February 2008 – guide price £30 per £100

3. On 11 January 2008 to buy the 5800 OneTouch with BetOnMarkets expiring on 25 January 2008 – guide price £10 per £100.

All of these bets did well out of the subsequent decline.

The 5800 OneTouch went to 100, for a 900% gain, on Monday 21 January. If I had been cleverer I could have bought a 5400 OneTouch at an even lower price! There again, £10 per £100 is an excellent risk/reward ratio and the further away I made the strike price the less were my chances of success.

I bought the 5800s on 11 January because it had then become pretty clear that the expected decline had begun.

I bought the NoTouches two days earlier because we had seen solid spike highs on the market. Elliott Wave Theory and price spikes (or *minus development* as they are known in Market Profile) form the backbone of my approach to markets. When we see a solid price spike, and that on the

9 January was a solid 50 points, we know that the extreme (meaning the price away from market action – in this case a high) is solid resistance and that the market is less likely to go there. That does not mean price will not go there but merely that it is less likely. A spike shows you price rejection (in Market Profile terms) and if price is rejected once it may well be again.

A trading idea

So there is one trading idea for you and let me spell it out.

Wait for a solid price spike and then buy a NoTouch beyond the extreme of the spike (the extreme away from current price action).

How long forward?

Deciding when the bet expires is a question of balance. You want the shortest term possible because that gives you the best chance of success.

But you also want the lowest price and the price goes lower the longer you make the time frame.

Where to set the price?

The key rule is: beyond the spike itself, but if there are also key support/resistance levels in the vicinity or any round numbers then it may pay to set the price beyond those as well.

And here is one more tip

BetOnMarkets is a great site but it always pays to compare prices. In 2007 BetsForTraders opened its website offering very similar bets. So always check prices on both sites.

In fact it does not stop there, recently I opened a bet with BetsForTraders, because their price was better, and then closed it with BetOnMarkets because they were then offering a much better price – in fact it was the 6408 NoTouch I mention above.

I hope this chapter provided food for thought.

Summary

In this chapter we have taken an in-depth look at a trading *campaign* which was built up over a period of some months and we then looked at specific binary bets which I used to trade the signals given.

In particular we have learnt about:

- The importance of options expiry
- Using Elliott to spot fast action
- How to use OneTouch and NoTouch bets

5.

Trading the News with Binaries

Traditional forms of trading can come unstuck when a major news item is coming out.

The markets can quickly go into "fast" mode, sometimes going in both directions (albeit not simultaneously) hitting any stops that may have been placed.

One way round this is to trade after the news. At major turning points the initial reaction to the news is often in the direction of the trend allowing the trader to enter at better prices against the trend. However this is fairly rare and it takes a fairly confident and determined trader to do this.

I'm sure every one reading this is confident and determined but it does not hurt to have an easier way to trade major news items.

Binary Bets are the answer and in many ways they are tailor-made for this situation. I say this because:

- Risk £100 and you can make £1000 – or multiples thereof

- Never get stopped out

- Trade before the news without fear

Binaries are a form of fixed-odds bet and if you bet on a 100 point fall and if that 100 point fall takes place then you win – the fact a 200 point rally came in first and the market then fell 300 points to give you your win does not matter a jot – you still win.

This makes life a lot simpler, it also means you can play both sides and win – maybe on both bets.

Example 5.1: Trading the news

To illustrate how this works I am going to go through a trade I recommended to my clients, and placed myself, on Wednesday 30 January 2008.

That was the day the Fed made an interest rate announcement but it was unusual because the Fed had cut rates already that month – an *emergency* 0.75% on Tuesday 22 January.

The question before the announcement was: would they cut again?

LunchTime Trader

Just before we go into the action itself let me just say a few words about *LunchTime Trader* (LTT). LTT is a service I run under the alias ADAM X. There are reasons for this and, to an extent, ADAM X is a composite character, but all the trading commentary and recommendations are mine.

This is a good example in that I got the news totally wrong but we still made good money on the trading.

I will now leave it to ADAM X, my alter ego, to take you through the bets we did that day and I will then explain this in more detail.

LTT – 11:55am Tuesday, 29 January 2008

Good Morning…

It could be time for the next move down.

If so it could be sharp, but we do have a US interest rate announcement tomorrow at 7:15pm. Apparently the market is already discounting a further 0.5% rate cut and this strikes me as fairly amazing.

If I were the Fed I wouldn't want to cut rates again so soon, as it would imply the situation was out of control. It would be like saying "Oh no, what do we do, nothing seems to work, let's cut rates again, and again, and again…"

As I've said before I don't think interest rates are going to solve this problem as it's 'principal' that's at stake and by 'principal' I mean the capital sum upon which the interest is based. That sum is a whole lot bigger and a whole lot more important than the interest. If you lend someone £100,000 to buy a house and the house falls to a value of £50,000 what is going to worry you is getting your £100,000 back not the, relatively trivial, interest element.

So I would announce, "No, we are not going to cut rates now as we want to monitor the result of the latest cut first, but we are very willing to cut rates at our next meeting!"

I, of course, am (I hope) far less qualified to judge these things, but I would only cut rates again if the situation was truly hopeless.

So, if they do cut rates, I would expect a knee-jerk blip UP, then a sustained fall as the markets digest the implied hopelessness of the situation.

[Looking back at this a few weeks later this is pretty much exactly what happened!]

If they don't cut rates – as I suspect – then we may see a knee-jerk blip down (maybe a big one) and then a more sustained rally.

Meanwhile the Elliott Wave pattern calls for new lows (i.e. the FTSE below 5338 and the Dow below 11634) and then a stronger rally.

That gives us plenty of food for thought with regard to tomorrow's action and beyond, but what of today?

I did think we may fall back, but I now think we may just dither around from here – although the US news on durable goods, released at 1:30pm, may have other ideas.

For now I plan to stand aside and keep an eye on the situation. If an opportunity arises, I'll be in touch.

That report set the scene and the following day I started to gear up to trade the news…

LTT – 12:34pm Wednesday, 30 January 2008

FTSE did dither about after my report yesterday and it's dithering some more today.

Indeed, it is likely to keep dithering into the close tonight as we wait for the all-important news from the US at 7:15pm. Will the Fed cut rates because the situation is truly hopeless or will they leave rates unchanged and face the market's anger as a consequence?

Whatever they do, there seems scope for some solid moves. Chart patterns suggest these moves will come into the downside but we cannot completely rule out upside moves and if we can find some low cost bets then we should go for them.

The daily bets on the FTSE that expire at 4:30pm this afternoon are not going to be much use to us in playing market moves in response to the US news, but the FTSE bets that open with IG at 5pm may be very useful.

These bets are based on tomorrow's action and expire tomorrow at 4:30pm. But there are no exotics (Tunnels, Hi/Los, and OneTouches) as these are only available when the underlying market is open. Nevertheless we have plenty of binary indices to play with.

My first thoughts are the *FTSE to finish up/down 50 points* (those are two separate bets: up and down) but I might consider the *FTSE to finish up/down 150 points* if they are cheap enough.

[Note: I was not suggesting these bets until after 5pm that day.]

My preference will be for the down bets but I will also buy the up bets if the odds are right.

We will also have the full range of bets on the Dow and I will be looking for a decent opportunity. The weekly bets on the Dow might also be useful.

I will get back to you after 4:30pm if I see something I like.

LTT – 5:48pm Wednesday, 30 January 2008

Good Evening.

FTSE went broadly sideways all day, as expected. It actually closed down 47 points which, in normal times, would be considered quite a big day. But we are not in normal times – far from it!

In less than two hours the Fed (at 7:15pm) will make an announcement which may (and probably will) have a big effect on markets in the short term.

I reckon the effect longer term will be around zero for two reasons:

1. Interest rates are governed by markets in the first place and not by Fed announcements.

2. I do not believe tinkering with interest rates is going to solve the problems on this occasion.

But as binary betters it is the short term that interests us and we want to find a bet that:

a) stands to do very well if we see sharp action, and

b) is cheap.

Looking at FTSE first the *FTSE to finish up/down 50 points* (those are two separate bets) are both priced to buy at around 40.

As we are not sure of direction and need to buy both that means a total cost of around 80 which is not too appealing. But here is one idea. Don't buy before the news. Consider buying *after* the news if one of those bets becomes very cheap.

Often you see knee jerk moves on news which are then totally reversed and such a move cannot be ruled out. But if you do a trade like this, keep it cheap and you will need to be watching the markets, hawk-like, as the news comes out.

The bets *FTSE to finish up/down 150 points* are both priced around 15 to buy so you could buy both for 30 and that makes some sense but there are no guarantees that we will see action that sharp and/or it may all be over by the time the Dow closes. So the Dow may shoot 200 points up, then shoot 200 points down but finish unchanged and FTSE may have a quiet day.

If you buy these bets and we do see sharp action after the news it may be worth closing the leg that benefits and leaving the other leg to run at, hopefully, zero cost.

Of course the ideal bets would be to **sell** the Dow Tunnels but the +200/-200 is only 54/59 and 200 points is a fair move.

Probably better to buy the two bets:

1). *Wall Street cash high to be >+200* – current price 10/14

2). *Wall Street cash low to be <-200* – current price 27/33

That way you may even win on both if it gets truly volatile although that is unlikely.

I appreciate there is quite a lot in this report but just choose one bit you are comfortable with and go with that.

The Wall Street Tunnel is probably the easiest bet but you may need to exit shortly after the news.

If you don't feel comfortable with any of the bets then I would suggest paper trading if you can. Choose a bet, check the price, write it down on a piece of paper and then see what happens. It's great practice."

So what happened next?

LTT – Thursday, 31 January 2008

Good Morning.

My expectation of the Fed's announcement proved totally wrong but, on the upside, my *TradeWatch* recommendations hit gold – which is, of course, what matters!

Plus I believe I got it totally right when I said "So if they do cut rates I would expect a knee-jerk blip UP, then a sustained fall as the markets digest the implied hopelessness of the situation."

Yesterday the Fed cut rates by another 0.5%, the Dow briefly saw a high over 200 points ahead (sending the Dow Tunnel and the "Hi" bet to a full profit – a return of over 600% on the cost of the "Hi" bet) and then promptly collapsed to end down on the day.

I think we saw the action of frightened men yesterday.

For many years now the governments of the Western world have been playing a high stakes game of pass the parcel and the trick is to pass the parcel to the next government, so that the financial time bomb inside the parcel doesn't explode all over your nice neat administration.

In the good old days, economies used to boom and bust and from the bust would arise, phoenix-like, a thrusting new economy.

But this could no longer be tolerated, especially as a succession of economists put into the inept hands of our politicians a variety of tools for prolonging the life of the old economy. Thus the old economy staggered on, limping and wheezing far beyond its normal productive life.

Maybe it is unfair to blame anyone for this – if you can achieve short-term good then people will tend to go for that option and let the longer term take care of itself.

But whatever the reasons, the financial time bomb gets bigger and more potent every time it is passed on, and eventually it was bound to go off.

I believe this is happening now and as the economy continues to unwind we will hit various economic black holes on the way down which will lead to more crises and more bad news, which will turn into a vicious self-feeding frenzy.

Not a pleasant thought – I hope I'm wrong!

But in the paper this morning that phrase, "economic black hole", was mentioned as a reason why the UK may need a 2% rise in income tax. It perfectly sums up the assumptions that seem valid in a time of boom but become disastrous in a time of bust.

Anyway, enough of this conjecture…

As I have already said, the US bets I recommended did well and I even made some profit on the UK bets.

These being the two bets *FTSE to finish up/down 150 points*, which I bought at a combined cost of 32.9 and got out at a combined price of 43.4. I sold the *up* bet at 7:24pm last night and the *down* bet earlier this morning."

Explaining the strategy

The chart patterns were not completely irrelevant in considering what strategy to adopt, but their input became irrelevant in the decision to back it both ways.

> Price is often a better guide than charts in this sort of situation. By *price* I mean the price of the bets.

The FTSE bets gave some profit advantage, but not much, and there is a clear logic why the Wall Street bets were better in any case.

This logic is that the news was coming out when the Dow was open, which gave two clear benefits:

1. It is immediately after the news that the wild gyrations may come in and this is what we are looking to capitalise on.

2. The exotic bets which expire when hit are only available when a market is open and it is these bets that are tailor made for this sort of situation.

These two points go hand in hand. I have talked about exotics elsewhere in this book but a wise man once told me that a good teacher must repeat the key points at least four times.

The key point with an exotic binary is that it can expire before its stated life. So a daily exotic may be expected to last until the end of the day (as any daily up/down bet would do) but all exotic binaries are bets on the underlying market reaching one or other pre-set levels – i.e. a OneTouch expires when that level is touched.

When key news comes out, what often happens?

We often see wild action that touches lots of levels a fair way off the levels before the news was issued. If we can pick up some cheap exotics we may be getting excellent value for our money. (The concept of value is another topic I plan to repeat a few times in this book!)

Compare this situation with our bets on FTSE where:

- We are unable to trade the exotics because these bets are only open when the underlying market is open.

- Because FTSE was closed when the news came out the wild gyrations might be long gone by the time it does open. Even if we do see a big opening gap it will be a distillation of the action – and often a very faded version!

In fact FTSE did fall heavily at the open but then rallied and ended up 42 points on the session. That early fall would have been magic if we had been able to buy exotics; but we could not and so the modest close was not great news for the *FTSE up/down >150 points* bets we had in place – albeit I closed those earlier.

Conclusion

In this chapter I have set out one unique aspect of binaries that make them a gift from heaven if you want to trade the news. Doing this is something I have found to be highly profitable and it has become a staple of the service I offer to *LunchTime Trader* clients.

As an aside I would add that writing in this way is a great way to really understand your strategies in the market. If I don't write, but merely think about my strategies, I find all sorts of illogical thoughts creep in. But write it down and you are *forced* to be logical – and you can learn a lot that way!

Summary

In this chapter we have taken an in-depth look at how to trade the news with binaries.

- Binaries allow us to trade without fear of either being stopped out or, alternatively, making a large loss.

- The wild gyrations following an important news item is often a gift for exotic binary traders.

- You will need to adapt your strategy to the situation in place ahead of the news.

6.

Trading the Waves with Binaries

One of the techniques I use in my trading is Elliott Wave Theory. In this chapter I want to tell you about the way I use Elliott to *read* markets and the binaries I then use to *trade* markets.

Elliott is my primary method of analysis and it allows me to make most of my forecasts. It is a fairly simple theory and consists of two basic principles:

1. **Impulsive action** consists of five waves (see following illustration)

2. **Corrective action** consists of either three waves or a more complex pattern

But in order to understand this we first need to define *impulsive* and *corrective*.

An *impulsive move* is one in the direction of the main trend and such a move is usually fast, direct and easy to classify.

A *corrective move* is contra-trend and tends to dither and dather, wibble and wobble. It is not easy to classify and generally if you are not sure what you are seeing it is more likely it is corrective.

Here is an Elliott five-wave impulsive rally.

Figure 6.1: Elliott five-wave impulsive rally

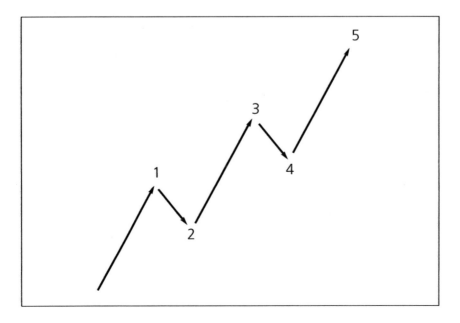

The Elliott fives should obey the following rules:

1. Wave 3 is never the shortest and is generally the longest

2. Waves 1 and 5 do not overlap.

3. Wave 2 and 4, which are *corrective* are generally of a different shape from each other (this is called *alternation*).

Elliott five in the real world:

Chart 6.1: FTSE hourly

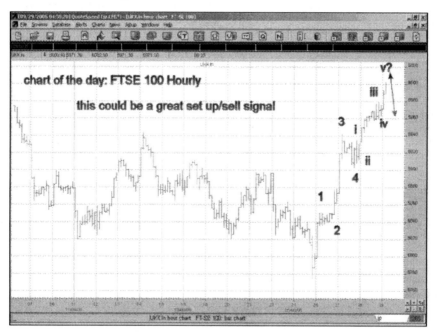

This chart is the same one shown in Chapter 6 of *Binary Betting*. I chose this because the five-wave pattern obeys all the key rules:

1. Wave 3 is not the shortest and may be the longest. We can, of course, check this but Elliott is principally a visual technique – at least it is the way I use it.

2. Waves 1 and 5 do not overlap.

3. Wave 2 and 4, which are corrective, are of a different shape from each other.

You may say,

> *but this chart does not look anything like your illustration!*

In some ways I would agree with you but a stylised illustration is always going to look different from real life. The key points are that we can count five waves and that the move obeys the rules.

The 1987 Crash

Now we will look at another real-life example[3].

Chart 6.2: FTSE daily

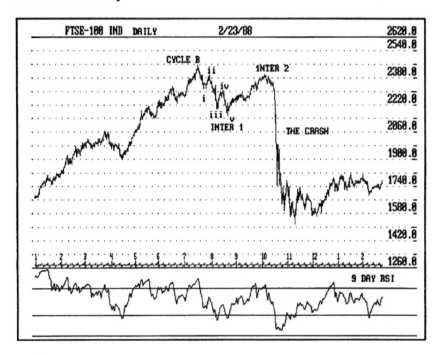

This chart goes back a few years but it is the best signal I have ever seen Elliott give.

From the peak labelled *Cycle B* you will see I have labelled the decline down to *Inter 1* as a i, ii, iii, iv, v move.

Yes, you can count five waves in declines as well as rallies!

---

[3] This example appeared in my first book *The Way To Trade*.

This brings us to the next point: Elliott waves are fractal – Elliott discovered chaos theory many years before anyone else!

The concept is simple but can seem confusing at first. Basically all the waves subdivide into "fives" and "threes" themselves. Here is a chart with waves 1 and 2 so subdivided.

Figure 6.2: An Elliott five with waves 1 and 2 subdivided

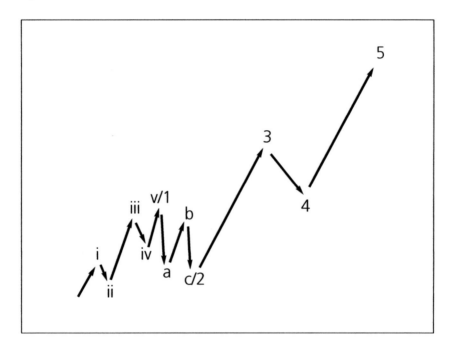

That looks a little complex but all I have done is subdivide waves 1 and 2 into their component parts. I could do the same with waves 3, 4 and 5 but I think the chart above is sufficient to make the point. You will notice how corrective wave 2 has been subdivided into a *three* – labelled a-b-c.

Trading the 1987 Crash

My first derivative trades were in 1985 and I then became a full-time trader in April 1987. As you will see from the chart I was expecting a big fall, but I have never claimed to have predicted a crash. Elliott led me to expect a fall in excess of 300 points but I was not expecting it to happen in one day!

Back in 1987 I was trading options and each FTSE option was worth £10 per point. I woke up on Monday 18 October 1987 with around twenty put options – £200 per point.

FTSE opened around 100 points lower and I closed the lot for a cool twenty grand – when twenty grand meant something.

But I do not look back on the Crash as one of my finest trading moments because the previous Thursday I had 60 put options in place – £600 per point.

Foolishly I closed out 40 of these on the Thursday expecting a bit of a bounce up when I could re-open. Big mistake as the hurricane hit the UK and on Friday the market was closed.

I did open some more via IG Index (I think one of my first trades with them) and bought some S&P options with Merrill Lynch – who wrongly advised me that they expired on the same date as FTSE (at the end of the month in those days). So my S&P options expired on the day I bought them – not much use for the Crash – although Merrill Lynch did buy me lunch to compensate!

Then to add to my woes I stared to sell puts into the Crash...

But that is another story and explains the lack of hair that remains to this day. At least I am still here to tell the tale!

Elliott hype and complications

I now need to say that I have adapted Elliott Wave Theory and taken from it what I find useful. Thus what I am talking about here is Elliott Wave *à la John Piper* – other texts will tend to differ. I am not claiming my version is better, merely that it suits me. So far I think there would be few disagreements between what you might call "standard" Elliott Wave Theory and my version, but as we get further into this that will change.

I do this with all the techniques I use. I have adapted commonly known methods and made them my own. So you will not find these precise techniques anywhere else.

I suggest you do the same: take what you find useful and make it your own.

I do have a fairly major problem with the way some people interpret Elliott and with the hype that is sometimes involved. Elliott is good for trading markets but it is also very good if you happen to write a market letter. Elliott often comes up with big forecasts and big forecasts sell subscriptions.

But let the marketing department loose on your advertising copy and it is not long before Elliott becomes a gift from the Gods, a technique that never fails. Now that kind of stuff is *dangerous* because it can fool traders into not using proper risk control and money management.

> If someone tells you that Elliott is always right then they are talking nonsense!

But the system does allow for many very complicated wave counts and in this way it can count all market action. To me this is useless, if the system accommodates everything a market may do then it loses all ability to provide good trading opportunities.

My version of Elliott Wave

I prefer to keep it simple. I really only look at two factors: impulsive and corrective action. If I can correctly identify which of these we are seeing then I can draw appropriate conclusions:

- If **corrective** I know that the main trend should resume shortly so I look for a signal that this is happening or has happened.

- If **impulsive** I know to trade with that trend and if we are in the fifth wave I know that we may get a contra-trend signal.

So my version of Elliott is a lot simpler than you may find elsewhere. But I would encourage you to do further research and reading a few books on Elliott is worthwhile. Even one good idea can reap a very healthy harvest. I allot time every day for research and would suggest at least one hour per day for this vital task.

But even in this simplified version there is still a fait bit to take in.

So far we have covered the basics. For the remainder of this chapter I am going to use real life examples, often linked to winning trades recommended by *LunchTime Trader*, to illustrate how I apply the principles of my version of the Elliott Wave Theory.

Here is the first one...

Chart 6.3: Two winning trades

The above chart formed the basis for two winning trades: the first on Friday 29 June 2007; and the second, the next session, on Monday 2 July. Spend a few minutes studying the chart.

Can you see the signals?

The key to this is the decline I have marked 1, 2, 3, 4 and 5. Once a move has seen five waves it is complete and we are due a rally (or a decline if it had been a five-wave advance) and that is the basis of the trades done on the following days.

I am going to mention one very important rule I use and this is that I want to see all the waves within a five to be roughly similar in terms of time. As a general rule, I would expect no wave to last longer than twice any other. At the same time you must be flexible. Applying Elliott Wave Theory is an art; it is not a mechanical process. If everything else is great but wave 4 is three times wave 1 in terms of time that may be acceptable.

Let me take you through this a step at a time so you can see exactly what I do.

First, do not try to force a wave count on the market. Just wait and you will find they develop all on their own.

Once you have seen a count, work out the implications. For example, in the chart above I knew to expect a rally and we saw this start from 5.

Having seen five waves down off a new high, as in this case, the implication is that we are now in a new downtrend, but this is not so relevant for shorter-term trading using binary bets.

We saw the first rally off the low (marked 5) and as a wave count always has a correction following an impulsive move I was looking for a pullback. Using Elliott I also knew that any such move would fail to make new lows – in other words it would be a buying opportunity.

We duly saw the pullback come in on 29 June (I have labelled this as a re-test) and if you look at the chart carefully you will see that the decline traced out an a-b-c form.

Trade 1

This was our buy signal and *LunchTime Trader* duly logged a £560 gain on this trade which only lasted a few hours. That gain was assuming a bet at £10 per point.

Trade 2

Trade 2 was all part of the same thing. I was on guard for the rally itself to be a correction. If we see five waves off the top it suggests a major trend change. In that aspect Elliott was wrong as we saw a very minor penetration to new highs on Friday 13 July. But even if it had been a correction the wave count argued for higher prices first.

So when we saw that a-b-c decline, marked on the chart at *Trade 2* – we went in again looking for a rally.

The rally did come in but we got out when the trade started to look uncertain. We will deal with this aspect of trading – taking profits and cutting losses – later in this book.

A look at the bets themselves

FTSE to finish up – 29 June 2007

Here is what I said in *LunchTime Trader* on Friday 29 June at 11:52am:

THE WEEKLY ROUND-UP

FTSE is down today and the first task for FTSE is to re-test Wednesday's low at 6496. I expect that level to hold although a small penetration is always possible. If it holds we should see a strong rally develop. Today's decline is the pullback I had expected to start yesterday but is now with us today.

Looking at FTSE, this decline may be over today and give us a buying opportunity.

But US markets are in a similar position and if the Dow falls back from 2:30pm-4:30pm then any rally on FTSE is not going to achieve very much.

Once FTSE has re-tested 6496 I expect a solid rally into the middle of next week. A gap opening to the upside is certainly on the cards for Monday morning. At last!

TradeWatch

[Bets I expect to win or give profit potential but which do not meet my risk parameters, at least not yet]

Tunnel prices remain fairly dire today and it doesn't look like we'll get any opportunities. The indications are that it may be a relatively brisk session with a fall first and then maybe a rally later.

But I will be looking at the *FTSE to finish up* bet today.

Both for the close today and for the close on Monday. FTSE looks very likely to move lower today and the question is whether it will then be able to rally strongly enough to get into positive territory before the close today.

If I think that is a reasonable bet I will recommend the trade. An alternative may be to buy *FTSE to finish up* after FTSE closes, if it gets cheap enough.

Another alternative may be to buy a NoTouch through www.BetOnMarkets.com and I will also be looking at this, although the time frame may be problematic.

So as you can see, there's a fair bit to watch today!

At 12:03pm I made it a formal recommendation to buy *FTSE to end up* at a price of around 14 – the bet closed at 100 that day for a gain on the risk involved of 614%.

To recap

I went for this bet because:

1. The Elliott pattern suggested more upside that day.

2. The initial decline gave us a good opportunity to get in *cheap*.

FTSE to finish up – 2 July 2007

The next session was on 2 July and here is my report that day which went out at 1:29pm.

No time to lose, this looks every bit as good as Friday's trade! So without further a do here's what you need to do.

Note: All recommendations are only good for the day.

TODAY'S TRADE – STONKER TRADE

BUY Binary indices – *FTSE to finish up* at 25 or lower. No Trade after 3pm. Type A bet – run to expiry or look to exit around 70.

This second bet did not work as well and I advised it be closed at around 50 – still a 100% gain on the risk involved.

Infallibility

A final, but important, point.

Elliott is not infallible, whatever anyone says. However carefully you work on the waves, not all your trades will win. I have to say this to counter all the hype that surrounds Elliott.

One pundit in the US who has written books on Elliott is convinced it is infallible. We used to exchange letters but I then committed the cardinal sin – blasphemy – when I questioned whether Elliott really was infallible. For this sin I was excommunicated and no longer received his letter.

Good thing really, as he pretty much completely missed the bull market from 1987-2000 as he was so sure Elliott was "right."

He even "proved" that it had not been a bull market at all by expressing the market in terms of the price of gold, or some such, and inflation adjusting. On that basis it was actually a bear market – but all the bulls weren't bothered, they had already banked their profits!

Anyway enough of the deluded. On to the next chart.

When a move fails to materialise

Chart 6.4: US Interest rate news, 18-19 September 2007

This was a particularly nice trade; again its roots lay in Elliott but there were other factors as we shall see.

The set-up here came in because the Elliott pattern up to the decline labelled a-b-c had been highly negative – I was looking for a big impulsive decline.

In the event all we got was that a-b-c – a fairly feeble corrective form.

This meant we had two signals indicating the market was going up instead. One in the form of the corrective nature of the decline, it counted as an a-b-c, and the second because our previous sell signal had not produced much – what does not go down, will go up (and vice-versa)!

> This brings us to an important point: when a move fails to materialise we look in the other direction.

On top of that we had the spike low (see chart); we will be looking at these in the next chapter. But this is another buy signal showing determined buying.

Then we had the form of the subsequent rally which I have labelled as 1, 2, i, ii meaning the fast action in the form of the third wave (remember these are generally the longest and also the fastest) was still to come.

Finally, and these were critical factors, the financial markets were in disarray because of the sub-prime mortgage crisis and the US was about to make an interest rate announcement – at 7:15pm, after FTSE had closed.

I reckoned the US was not going to upset markets and this made it an odds-on bet that the announcement would be positive.

But using binary bets I could get much better odds than that and recommended the net *FTSE to end up >50 points* at around 30. This had odds of over 2 to 1.

With all these factors going for it this bet should have been a winner.

And it was!

> This is what I was talking about regarding *value bets*. If I can get 2 to 1 on a bet that should be evens I will be betting all day!

After the interest rate news came out (rates down 0.5%) the bet was priced at around 60 and it closed at 100 the next day.

I should mention that IG quote prices 24 hours on most bets and I was able to buy this bet after 5pm on Tuesday (after FTSE had closed for that day) but based on and expiring at Wednesday's close. FTSE was actually up over 150 points on Wednesday.

My *LunchTime Trader* commentary on this bet

This formed part of my report on 18 September 2007 at 4:22pm

TODAY'S TRADE

FTSE has rallied quite well today and the Dow is also well up. These factors have driven the prices of the up bets higher and the opportunities are not as abundant as I had hoped. In fact I am even feeling a little contrary and feel like buying a down bet as well, as insurance.

It also seems that good news is widely expected.

Nevertheless, there is a strong case for arguing FTSE to make further progress towards 6400 and I recommend the following trade.

We are buying this trade this evening, before the US interest rate announcement at 7:15pm – it is based on FTSE's close tomorrow (Wednesday).

TRADE

Buy Binary Indices – *FTSE to finish up >50 points*. Run to expiry or look to exit around 80.

Bet – Buy Binary Indices – *FTSE to finish up >50 points*. As FTSE closed today at 6283.3 this bet will be winner if FTSE closes above 6333.3 tomorrow. FTSE closes at 4:30pm, and an auction is held a few minutes later to determine the closing price.

Price Guide – buy around 32 or lower but trade is live once alert issued at price. I trade at win or lose, I do not recommend buying above 42.

Current Price – IG 21/26; CS no quote.

LunchTime Trader – 19 September 2007

On 19 September I sent this out at 10:01am

Good morning and I hope you got on to the trade yesterday evening.

After the alert I bought at 28.4 although lower prices were available earlier to those who followed the recommendation in *TradeWatch*.

We are now going to take profits and the current price on IG is 81/85; CS 80/86.

I think it is highly likely this bet will expire at 100 when FTSE closes tonight but I am not comfortable holding a bet priced at 80+ all day just in case. To me it means risking 80+ to make 20 or less and I do not like those odds.

But I know many people do like these odds and even open bets at those odds.

It is all about your trading personality and the way you do things. Good traders discover their successful trading personality and go from there.

Today I would not sell at less than 80 and that is my recommendation. Many of you may already have done this as the bet has been above 80 for most of the morning.

For those with accounts both with IG and CS you may find the CS price more stable as we were unable to open the bet on CS last night. If you sell the bet on CS you will be left with a *buy* on IG and a *sell* on CS both of which will expire at the close. There may also be arbitrage opportunities.

Once the alert is out I will sell at 80+ and that will crystalise the trading result.

LunchTime Trader – 20 September

Finally I sent out the Trade Review on 20 September at 11am

Okay, here's the second of today's blasts, this time going through the winning trade we enjoyed yesterday.

Here's what I recommended:

Buy Binary Indices – *FTSE to finish up >50 points*. Run to expiry or look to exit around 80.

This was a winning trade – so well done us!

After the alerts went out I bought at 28.4 and closed this morning at 85.8. The results are as follows:

Cost: 28.4
Total cost/risk: £113.6 (28.4 x £4)
Exit: 85.8
Profit: 57.4 points
Cash profit: £229.60 (57.4 x £4)

One of the things I really like about this service is when one of our members takes my comments and decides to do something different.

One of us decided to buy the bet *Wall Street to close up 300 points* – this bet was priced at around 5 yesterday afternoon and closed at 100.

Another found that the bet *FTSE to close up >50 points at 12pm* was at a better price after the alert went out and bought that instead. That bet also expired at 100.

I have said before that the more you put into this, the more (money and fun) you will get out of it – this illustrates the point!

Conclusion

That completes a basic introduction to Elliott Wave although I will be referring to this as we review further trading examples and charts throughout this book.

Right now your task is to start looking at charts and counting the waves – I assure you it can be a very profitable way to spend some time and it's also fun!

Finally here are a few suggestions of how you might surf the (Elliott) waves:

1. Third waves are the most dynamic and it is during a third wave that the further out bets like *FTSE to end up >150 points* might come good; and these bets are generally very cheap. But don't necessarily go so far

out, also check out *FTSE to end up >50 points* and *FTSE to end up >30 points* plus the Hi/Lo bets. Remember if you are in a *down wave* you will be looking to bet that FTSE will be down, not up.

2. Once the fifth wave is complete, up or down, think about what sort of move we might see and bet accordingly.

3. The same applies when corrections look to be over. Ferret out the bets that will win once the main trend resumes.

4. Sometimes FTSE gives two clear alternatives but by using *Tunnel* bets you can often make money whichever of those comes good.

Summary

In this chapter we have learnt:

- The basics of how I use Elliott Wave Theory

- The five-wave form

- Corrective and impulsive action

- How to interpret the waves

- How to trade (surf) the waves

7.

Trading the Spikes

I think every trader has to develop the techniques he or she uses and make them his or her own. This is what I have done with Market Profile.

Yes, I know I am repeating myself but I covered that early on – repetition is an important aspect of imparting knowledge!

Market Profile

I started to use Market Profile in the 1990s when I was introduced to it by an institutional trader. The approach was developed by Peter Steidlmayer who had the idea of applying a Victorian method of statistical analysis – the bell curve – to the markets. What he found was quite staggering. Many days markets traced out a distribution to form a perfect bell curve – see the illustration below.

Figure 7.1: The bell curve

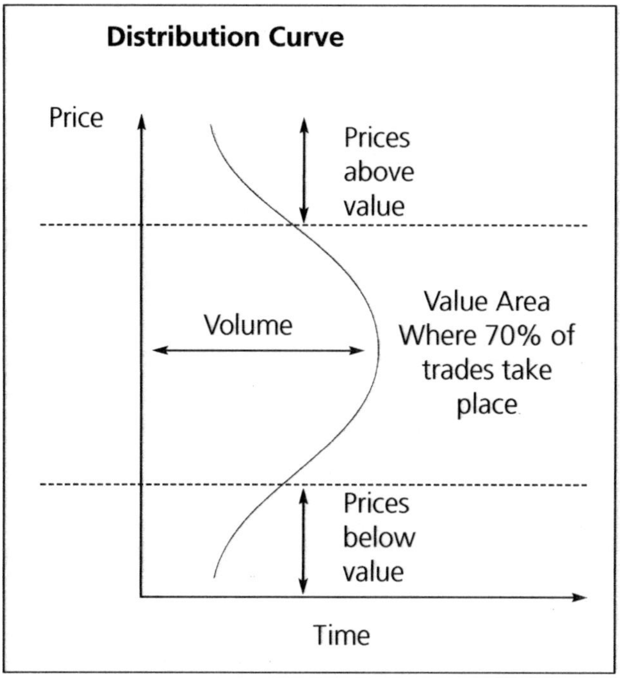

Source: Stocks and Commodities magazine

The above is a classic bell curve; it is *fat* in the middle and *thin* at the ends. The fatness is caused by volume but not in the normal sense.

Volume is normally how many shares or futures contracts (£s per point for spread betters) are traded over a day; but in the case of Market Profile *volume* is defined as how long the market you are tracking sees a certain price.[4]

If you take a typical bell curve, as in the illustration above, you will see that the market spends most of its time in the central area and less time at the extremes. If you watch market action it is quite often that we see price move to an extreme and then buyers or sellers come in and swiftly knock it back.

Spike anatomy

This is an important concept in my trading and it is called *rejection*. When I see this it is a signal that the market wants to go in that direction. I will explain this in detail:

The market moves quickly outside the day's range – although this can also be an opening move. If you are looking at a bar chart you will see this as a spike, although whilst it is forming you will not know whether it will continue.

For the sake of this discussion we will assume the move came in to the downside and that it moves around 15 points below the body of the day's action (i.e. the fat bit on the market profile chart).

At that point we would have a sell signal on the chart. Critically, a number of traders will have placed stops below support (such stops would exercise risk control on long spread bets) and will be stopped out by the move. As a binary trader you do not need stops as binaries come with built in risk control (a point you should be fully aware of by now!)

However this fall brings in some solid buying. This is the critical part of the equation, unless we see that solid buying all we have seen is a break of support – a clear negative.

The solid buying pushes price back into the body of the action.

---

[4] This is explained in a lot more detail in Chapter 14 of *The Way to Trade* which is included in the appendix to this book.

Spike analysis

So what have we seen?

There are various answers to this question.

It may just have been a stop hunting party. There are many, many ways to make money in the markets and one of these is to set out to hit other traders' stops. You need a certain amount of fire power to do this as it means pushing price below a key level (where we all know the stops lurk). But once there, the stops will be hit and traders will be selling the market – meaning you can buy back your shorts at a profit – lubbly jubbly!

But if it is a solid spike – and experience will tell you which is which – it is an excellent buy signal. Especially so if it points in the direction of the trend. If we see a spike low that confirms the uptrend.

It is not strictly relevant to binary trading but if you consider the position of those who would have got stopped out by the spike (and this will happen whether it was a stop hunting party or not) you will realise that they have been stopped out by the very thing which confirms that the trade was right. The way to avoid this rather ridiculous situation is to use *time* stops which you only trigger if the market spends sufficient time beyond your mental stop point (you cannot place time stops in the market). Spikes, generally being fairly rapid affairs, tend to spend only a little time beyond such levels but this is not always the case and some are very big – 40 points or more – so time stops are not a *complete* solution. In fact the nature of markets tends to mean there are never any *complete* solutions.

Trading spikes on news

I want to make one final point and this concerns spikes linked to news items. Successful traders are a highly risk-averse bunch. If they weren't they would not be successful over the longer term. Often a market has gone as far as it is going to go in one direction but there is a key news item due. All eyes are on this announcement. The smart money knows the market is due to reverse but they want to get the news out of the way first. Let's say the market has been falling for some weeks and is deeply over-sold. The news comes out and it is truly terrible!

What happens?

The smart money waits while the market does its normal knee-jerk thing and falls even more. Then the smart money piles in and you get a solid buying response on *bad* news.

This is one of the strongest signals you can get and in an earlier chapter we looked at how binaries can be uniquely useful when trading the news (I bought a new Porsche from the profits of one such trade!)

Spike signals

We will now look at a number of examples of good spike signals.

Note: I have studied Market Profile, become familiar with all it has to offer and then selected one part which I find useful in my trading. As you should know by now I recommend you do the same with every technique you use – you may find you prefer other parts than those used by the majority of traders.

Chart 7.1: Elliott, spikes and the news

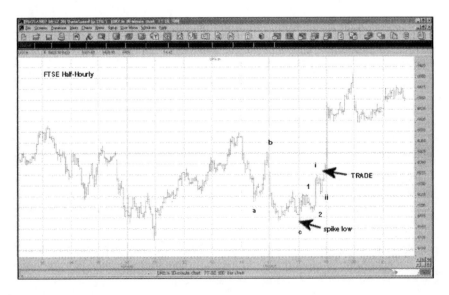

The chart opposite is one we have already looked at in a previous chapter. This trade incorporates Elliott, spikes and the news!

You will see that I have marked the spike low on this chart. In this case we saw the market probe lower right from the off (on 18 September) and this action was below all of the price action from the previous day. The close on Wednesday 17 September had been at 6182.8 and FTSE saw a low some 20 points lower at 6158.8 within a few minutes of the open at 8am. But minutes later FTSE was back in positive territory.

The lower price had brought in determined buying, plus it was early in the session and this is also an important point. Only determined traders go in early. Other less determined traders tend to follow on and watch what happens first.

That spike low set the scene for the whole 350+ point rally that followed – but you would have had to be up fairly early in the morning to catch it!

Here is another chart.

Chart 7.2: More spikes

This chart also covers the key action from the previous chart. You will see that all of the key turning points on this chart are spikes – that should tell you something about the importance of this particular technique.

However it is the spike high on 19 September 2007 that I want to talk about; this formed the basis of a trade on 25 September (I also recommended this to subscribers of my binary betting service on that day). Here are the key factors:

The spike high came in near the close on 19. It also constituted a failed break above the key level of 6500 (I will be looking at failed breaks and failed re-tests in a later chapter). When a market goes above a key level this can be a solid buy signal. If it then gets knocked back with vigour, as in this case, it becomes a solid sell signal – especially if it also qualifies as a spike.

The initial move off the spike was not impressive and the market dithered for a while and then tried to regain 6500. But it failed and this added to the signal, as did the opening action on 25 September.

In fact the opening spike on the 25th is an example of one of the more important trading signals on an intraday basis (i.e. within the day itself). In all cases you trade away from the spike extreme and in this case it was an extreme high suggesting short positions.

FTSE futures and cash

One point that I need to mention relating to that spike on 25 September is that it did not appear on the futures chart. The FTSE cash is a mathematical calculation based on the top 100 companies quoted in the UK (not necessarily based in the UK) and is not directly traded. The FTSE cash always opens at the previous closing level. The FTSE futures are different and are directly traded and will open where the market is expected to be at that time.

I treat a spike as being stronger if it appears on both charts: futures and cash. The reason for this is time. The key attribute about a good spike is that it is formed quickly showing determination. A spike on the cash chart has all night to form and so the essential element of quick formation may be missing.

FTSE duly fell back but we saw a solid bounce off the low at 6367.

In fact it was another spike!

I closed off my positions at that point – this sort of action is important when taking profits and cutting losses.

The trade I recommended on *TradeWatch* that day was the *FTSE cash low to be <-100* (this bet goes to 100 if FTSE sees a low more than 100 points from the prior close) the prior close in this case was that on the 24th at 6465.90.

FTSE failed by 2 points to send this bet to the full 100 but the recommendation gave what I call *good profit potential*. When I sent out the report the bet was priced at 34/40 and it moved into the high 90s so those looking to take profits had plenty of chance.

Nailing the Spikes

Finally, here are a couple of suggestions of how you might *nail* the spikes:

1. A spike is a clear signal that the market is due to move away from the extreme made by the spike, so **consider selling a OneTouch beyond the spike**. By selling a OneTouch you are creating a bet some companies call a no-touch! For example FTSE saw a spike low at 6507 on 4 October 2007 and the 6500 OneTouch could have been sold for around 70.

2. Alternatively, **treat a spike low as a buy signal and a spike high as a sell signal**. Look for bets that will benefit as the market rallies or falls away. I gave some examples under this section in the previous chapter.

Summary

In this chapter we have learnt about price spikes – which I consider to be one of the most important trading signals that any market throws out.

In particular, we have:

- Looked at Market Profile and the bell curve

- Looked at specific examples

- Learnt how these signals can be traded

8.

Trading Failures, the Mind of the Market and Trendlines

We are now going to look at the other market techniques I use.

Failed re-tests and failed breaks

These are known by a number of names, such as double bottoms, double tops, W and M formations (they look like these letters) – and "that goddamn signal" by those who lose money! But I prefer *failed re-tests* and *failed breaks* because I believe the two signals are different and also because it can be highly significant to Elliott Wave patterns whether we see the one or the other.

For example, if we are looking for an Elliott five to develop but wave 5 fails to exceed the peak of wave 3 (a failed re-test) then it is not much of a five – in fact it counts better as a corrective a-b-c. The illustration below shows this.

Figure 8.1: Failed re-test

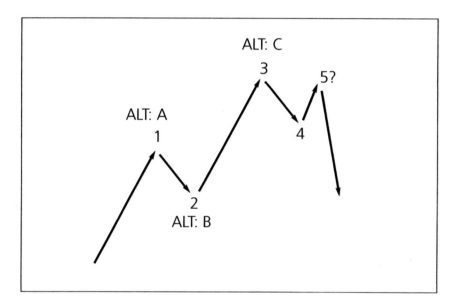

The illustration shows a failed re-test; the key point is that the market tries to regain the previous high but fails to do so.

Pretty much all of the techniques I use work both ways. By this I mean they work both as buy or sell signals and are completely reversible in this respect. Turn the above illustration on its head and it becomes a buy signal.

The only real difference is that markets tend to fall more quickly than they rise – and they do this because fear (and her ugly sister, panic) are stronger (being impulsive) than greed which is more of an emotion.

We will now look at a failed break.

Figure 8.2: Failed break

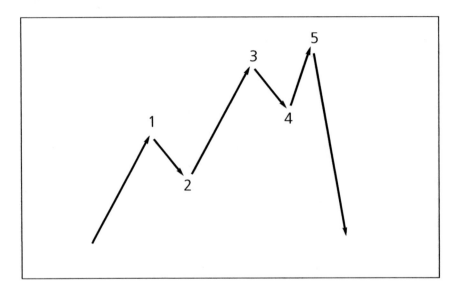

In this illustration wave 5 goes higher than wave 3 but the market falls back – as the fifth wave is the last in the sequence. I call this a *failed break* as the market breaks higher but then fails and we fall back.

> The key difference between a failed break and a failed re-test is that a break means that the support or resistance represented by the previous extreme is penetrated, but with a failed re-test it is not.

I must also add another important point. I have linked both these signals with Elliott because that is my primary market technique, but we see many failed re-tests and failed breaks where we have no clear Elliott patterns.

We will now look at a chart giving a few examples.

Chart 8.1: Examples of re-tests

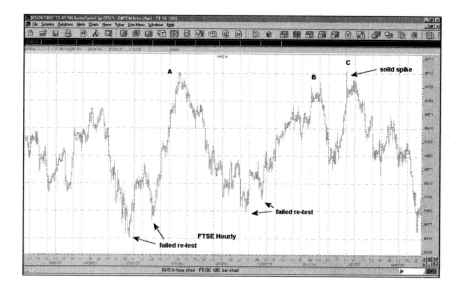

You will see I have marked two failed re-tests at the lows and in both cases we see the market make an initial low, rally, and then move back to test the previous low.

Why does it do this?

The mind of the market

The market's function is to maximise trade – that is why it was created and it is how the people who run the market get the most cash out of it by way of fees and commissions. In order to maximise trade the market needs to visit areas where trade exists – a good example is those stop hunting parties I mentioned earlier. Stops are placed and they are an "intent to trade". OK, the people who place the stops don't want them to get hit as they would much prefer to make some money (or more money) from the trade. But the market (and I mean this in the widest sense as the market is composed of all the people who participate in it) knows where most of those stops are and, in its bid to maximise trade, it goes and finds them. Yummy, more trade for the market!

But it is also true that that there will be plenty of *trade* to be done if the market re-visits key highs and lows. In the case of lows, as shown on the chart above, there will be bulls who saw the buying when the market went up the first time and are keen to get in at similar prices. Then there will be the bulls who got in too high in the previous rally (these are called weak holders) who get stopped out by the fall. Plus there will be bears, who think the previous downtrend is continuing, who sell the move.

You may wonder why I am at pains to explain why these moves happen; this is because I try to *get into the mind of the market*! I also believe that if you understand *why* something happens, you will be far better placed to use that move to make money.

Throughout this book I do my best to tell you not only the important patterns and indicators to look out for but also why they work for this very reason.

Failed break

To return to the chart the key point is the high I have marked as "C" – this is a failed break above both points "A" and "B". It is also a spike high which adds to the strength of the signal. As explained earlier, a failed break is where price goes beyond the previous extreme, in this case higher than the highs seen at points "A" and "B."

Failed breaks are generally stronger than failed re-tests.

Why should this be?

It does not seem logical in that you would expect strong action to form a failed re-test, meaning sellers would come in below the high (or above the low) thus creating a failed re-test and not a failed break.

In fact this is a valid point and it is important to realise that any explanation of market action is always going be incomplete. Death, war, catastrophe, fat-finger syndrome, unexpected news and a wide range of other factors can influence price and create or destroy patterns.

But this is relatively rare and the reasons why these patterns form, and their significance, remains an important aid to the money-making process.

Failed breaks form for the same reasons as failed re-tests – they simply go a little further.

Above I set out what happened in the case of lows. With highs like point "C" there will be bears who saw the selling when the market went down the first time and are keen to get in at similar prices. Then there will be the bears who sold too low in the previous decline (these are again called weak holders) who get stopped out by the rally. Plus there will be bulls who think the previous uptrend is continuing and buy the move correspondingly.

The balance between those long and short

To explain why a failed break is a stronger signal we must look at one of the basic market mechanisms and this is that the direction of the market is governed by the number of people who are long and short.

It is easiest to understand this point at major extremes.

Take New Year's Eve 1999. On 30 December 1999 (the last session of the year), FTSE peaked at 6950 and as I write that level has never been equalled. With 2008 bringing in solid falls it could be decades before FTSE sees that level again.

At that extreme in 1999 there was not a cloud in the sky plus it was New Year's Eve with all the positive emotion that brings to the party – a celebration of the year just gone, although in 1999 it was not just the year, but the decade and the century and the millennium. There was certainly a lot to celebrate if you think of all that mankind had accomplished in the last 1000 years! Then add in all the optimism for the coming year, the coming decade, the coming millennium.

Do you think this is not relevant?

The market is, in one sense, a *maelstrom* of human psychology and it is very much how we feel that determines price.

Never forget:

    Price = Value x Sentiment

To return to our main point, the turn comes when sentiment is so positive that everyone is positioned one way – they have all bought the market.

When this is the case what can happen?

Only one thing. If everyone has bought the market, it has to go down.

Who is left to buy?

And all those who have bought are all potential sellers as the market heads on down.

What has this got to do with failed breaks I hear you cry?

The answer is that it has to do with the consensus, how many people are long or short. With a failed break of this sort, meaning a break to new highs, there would be traders who are short who will be stopped out – that adds to the consensus. There will also be traders who go long on the break to new highs (which is a buy signal) and that will also add to the consensus.

Another important point is that it is the moves which are unexpected which tend to be the strongest – in this context Crashes are *never* expected. A failed break is a bigger surprise than a failed re-test.

I may have said too much on this point but I think it important to understand how markets work and the actual mechanics behind the price action we see. This point has importance in that context.

Here are two suggestions of how you might turn these failures into success:

1. A failure is a clear signal that the market is due to move away from the double top or bottom (and is just like a spike in this respect), so consider selling a OneTouch beyond the highs or lows – by selling a OneTouch you are creating a bet some companies call a NoTouch.

2. Alternatively treat these failures as buy or sell signals. Look for bets that will benefit as the market rallies or falls away.

The mind of the market and news

The market is a psychological maelstrom formed of all the traders and investors who participate in it.

How do we see into its mind?

We do it by selecting a focus. We focus on a few key aspects and we become expert in the application of those key aspects. So far I have told you about the news, Elliott Wave, price spikes, and failed re-tests and breaks.

These are my chosen focus and I have stripped them down to the basics so I can apply my techniques in seconds. It is not about saving time although it does do that. It is about making everything simpler so that you can become an expert – far easier to become an expert in a few chosen fields than in the mass of market information that is out there.

Your focus defines you as a trader and it also defines your success.

> When it comes to the mind of the market there is a great mass of information and you have to choose key aspects which are going to be useful because most of it is pretty useless in reality.

This technique is, again, news-based but only when it creates an unexpected reaction.

If we see good news and the market goes up it does not mean very much. But, say, if we see good news and the market goes down – now that can mean a great deal! If that happens, you get a clear insight into the mind of the market. The market is telling you that it is poised to go down.

Bear in mind that all we want to know about the *mind of the market* is whether it is going to go up or down. A fairly basic question – we are not too interested in the market's thoughts on quantum mechanics or whether or not there is a God!

I touched on this earlier when I was talking about the smart money waiting for the news to be out before piling in – that is an example of when you may see this sort of action.

It does not happen every day but when it does it can be an excellent signal.

Binaries and news

One of the great benefits of binaries is that risk is always tightly controlled. This is especially important when a key news item is about to come out and we looked at this in detail earlier. Usually, if you are spread betting, the best advice is to stay well clear of news because sudden sharp moves can be expensive, especially if your stops are not guaranteed! But with binaries you can only lose your stake. Of course you do not want to lose your stake but you have to match that risk with the potential reward.

Trendlines

Trendlines can be extremely useful. Here is an example:

Chart 8.2: Trendlines

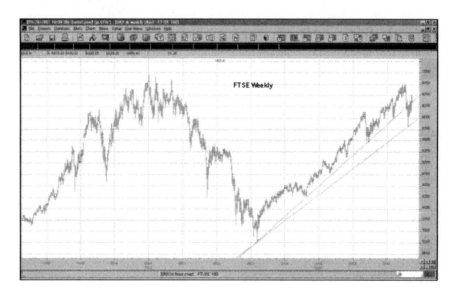

Look at the higher of the two straight lines on this chart. A trendline is drawn by connecting two points and you can see how the line goes through the first two lows. At that point you cannot be sure that the trendline is going be of any relevance – it is only when your trendline is "documented" (meaning it acts as support or resistance for future highs/lows) that you know you have a good trading reference.

The upper line above has been "documented" a number of times. I count six times (including the first two) and that level of documentation makes that a formidable line.

As this is an up-trendline, meaning it points upwards and links together a series of lows, then one useful technique is to buy the market whenever it gets near that line. If you had done this once the line became established you would have had four good buying opportunities – I'm not counting the first two as the line cannot be drawn until they are in place.

On each instance you would have risked a little (representing the difference between your entry on/just above the line and your stop somewhere below the line) and, as you can see from the chart, your potential gains would have been excellent each time.

We are now going to look at the same chart but with a difference:

Chart 8.3: Trendline channel

Can you spot what is different, not with the trendlines, but with the chart itself?

There are various ways of using trendlines and this one is known as a *trend channel*. You will see that the two lines are parallel and that the market has bounced between them for several years.

With a trend channel you can buy the market when it gets near the lower trendline and sell it when it goes near the upper trendline.

Have you spotted the difference yet?

It is not an easy one, nor obvious. But this chart is drawn on a logarithmic scale. That means that a 100% gain will look the same whether the market moves from 100 to 200, 2500 to 5000, or 5000 to 10,000. Such a scale has little difference over shorter-term charts but over time it has a fundamental difference.

On this chart the difference is not vast but it is significant. If you look at the break below the trendline towards the right of the chart you will see that on the first chart we have seen a clear break back above the trendline but on the second chart this is nowhere near as positive – it could just be an attempt to break through that fails.

Should you use a logarithmic scale or not?

I don't think it matters too much. The important thing is to find trendlines that are well documented.

Finally, a few words about two additional techniques.

Failed signals

If you get a clear signal but the market does nothing or you only see a fairly feeble move then you have another glimpse into the mind of the market. When this happens you often get a solid move the other way.

Moving averages

I want to say a bit about moving averages – a lot of technical analysis started with this simple technique.

Chart 8.4: Moving averages

The above chart is very short term (a 1 minute chart on the Dow). I have overlaid two moving averages – the 13 minute and the 21 minute. I chose these numbers fairly arbitrarily, although they are part of the Fibonacci series. I also chose the day arbitrarily – it just happened to be the chart of the Dow on the day I was writing this section.

The system is that you buy or sell as the two moving averages cross and you can see that it works fairly well. Although do bear in mind that the signals are given after the move has started so you would not be trading at the best levels.

Looking at the signals above I would say you have two good profits, one exceptionally good, two losses and one breakeven.

If you decided you wanted to use a system like this you would need real time pricing software.

Summary

In this chapter we have learnt:

- The basics of failed re-test and failed breaks
- How to trade these signals
- How to look into the "mind of the market"
- The basics of trendlines
- The concept of failures
- How to use a simple moving average trading system

Part III – You and Your System

9.

How Many Brains do you Think you Have?

If a giant python slithered its way into your bathroom as you played with your rubber duck would you:

1. think through the logistics of how it got there

2. feel a warm glow as you admire the rich colours of the snake and the way in which the light gleams on its pointed fangs

3. get the hell out of there as quickly as possible – naked though the window if need be!

Whichever action you choose would mean using one of your three brains.

The human brain is a complex beast that has formed over millions of years. The instinctive part of the brain, the brain stem, came from our reptilian ancestors. The limbic system (emotional part) derives from our basic mammal heritage and is also very ancient. Of more recent vintage in the neo-cortex which involves reflective thought processes and imagination.

These three brains are not that well co-ordinated at this point in human development!

This does vary from individual to individual and there are those who have taken time and care to improve the situation for themselves. To become successful as a trader may require just that.

Figure 9.1: Stylised model of the human brain

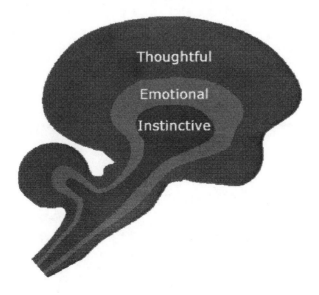

Although we use all three of our brains, we each tend to have one brain which we rely on the most. Those who are thoughtful will tend to become more adept at logic and thus do better in IQ tests. Those who are emotional will tend to develop a higher emotional intelligence (EQ) which tends to be a better guide to success than IQ. Those who are instinctive will become more intelligent in that way and possibly end up as professional sportsmen and women earning a lot more than the rest of us.

It is all too easy to become elitist if one excels at one or other aspect of brainpower but I suspect we all have very similar capacities – we simply channel them differently. The intelligence that David Beckham exhibits with a football may seem very different to that which Mozart brought to his musical compositions but who is to say which is the "better" genius? Albeit Mozart chose a more long-lasting medium whereas Beckham's moves are over almost before they have begun.

Why can't we all excel in our own chosen fields?

This question is a large part of what this chapter is all about and the chosen field in question is binary (and fixed-odds) trading.

I will start with the two biggies: commitment and emotional intelligence.

Achieving anything at a high level is not easy. As you get better and better at what you do the competition becomes tougher and tougher until you are playing for England in the World Cup, or composing for the king.

At the same time as the competition gets tougher the temptations become more and more appealing, which is where emotional intelligence comes in.

There are all too many examples of those who have made it to the top only to fail at that point and many more who stumble on the way. To name a few: George Best, Amy Winehouse, Syd Barrett, Jim Morrison, Jimmy Hendrix, Janis Joplin, Pete Dougherty, Michael Barrymore, Victor Neiderhoffer, Nick Leeson and Kurt Corbain.

Those few provide a good range of people who have found success too hot to handle or who have stumbled on the way. Many on the list are accepted genii in their field and there does seem a high proportion of people who reach the peak of their profession but do not handle it very well. Does genius bring with it its own problems or does it cause isolation in those who have it? Do the problems themselves drive the individual on to do the incredible? Is it the disappointment of reaching the top and realising that all that cash, adoration, and fame have not made a jot of difference to the problems that may have driven you there in the first place?

But I am getting ahead of myself and want to go back to the markets and where it all began – with the decision to enter the markets.

Which of your brains do you think you use when deciding it is time to trade?

We enter the most competitive arena that exists on this planet and we know that we are going to compete directly with experienced traders who have been doing this for years. We also know that the game is rigged and that every time we trade we are going to pay a spread the size of which makes any casino green with envy.

Yet we carry on regardless confident in the thought that we will win.

That does not seem a very logical action to me!

Therefore, my belief is that the decision to trade is almost invariably an emotional one, not a thoughtful one.

Why do we trade?

Is money really what we want when we enter the markets? Or is it excitement, fun, prestige and self-esteem?

Many of the traders I have coached over the years have been successful in other fields. They may be doctors, dentists, solicitors, businessmen and accountants. In most case they have done well but their work has ceased to be a challenge and they want more in their lives.

This is the emotional brain at work and the important point is that the motivation which takes us to the trading arena in the first place will also be the trigger when we actually take a trade.

Let's take the example of a man who is bored with his work. He wants more in his life and decides trading is the thing. It sounds profitable, fun and it will give him something to boast about at the golf club.

But he comes to trading because he is bored.

Guess what?

He will trade when that kicks in – he gets bored and thinks (with one of his brains): *this is why I got into the markets.*

BANG! – he trades.

Trading done in this way will not usually make money consistently as it will be too random – of course the market will throw in the occasional winner just to confuse the situation.

Now it may not be boredom. Maybe it is self-esteem. I discovered this some years ago after I had had an argument with my wife. I found myself trading for no good reason. I realised that the argument had caused a self-esteem *blip* and I had traded to restore my equilibrium.

It is all too easy to do this without realising it unless you use a totally mechanical system, which is why I believe that using such a system at some point in your trading career is essential. How else to see those stray thoughts, instincts and emotions at work?

The point I have just made goes to the core of many of the trades we do – ignore it at your peril!

There again, if you are getting emotional rewards for your trading you may be quite happy with the situation, albeit at a subconscious level.

At this point it is important to distinguish between those who are very happy with trading as a hobby and those who want to make money. The *hobby* trader is not too bothered if it costs a bit of cash over the year as the sheer thrill of it all outweighs that – it is fun, exciting, and gives plenty to talk about, especially the winners. Those who want to make money are different; they treat this as a business which means hard work and commitment.

How your three brains work with the markets.

The three brains:

- The **impulsive brain** is prone to the *flight or fight* syndrome and is prone to take action, almost without you knowing it, at certain points – in particular when seeing fast action against you.

- The **emotional brain** will take action when it needs a fix.
- The **thoughtful brain** will think it is in control (but this chapter should dispel that complacency fairly quickly).

But even if the thoughtful brain is in control

1. How much does it really understand about the markets?

2. How much testing has it done of all those beliefs which underlie your trading approach?

3. How much testing has it done on the system you are using now?

All of these are key questions that have a direct bearing on your profits or losses. If you are making money then you may feel you do not need to be too concerned with these questions. But if you are not, they may be the key to future success.

Our three brains are also fully at work once we are positioned.

We log on to www.BetOnMarkets.com and we decide FTSE is going up and buy the 6600 OneTouch which runs for one month. With FTSE at 6400 the bet costs £670 to win £1000. FTSE starts to fall away…

What do we do?

Most people bury their heads in the sand at this point.

You see, all through our lives we have been taught to grab the good stuff and we have spent hours learning how to get it. We are not very used to failure. Not that losing money in the markets on one trade is a failure – it is simply business as usual – it is only failure if you lose overall. But it is important to cut your losses, and if you let them run you are not going to come out on top.

This is an emotional response.

We don't *like* losses, they make us miserable, so we ignore them.

But we *do* like profits, we like them lots! So let's take the same bet. We buy at 670 and FTSE rallies. Our bet is now worth 810.

Too tempting – we grab the profit.

It is never good to run losses but our *emotional* brain can easily do this as it wants to ignore the losses. But we have to run profits, otherwise we will never cover our losses, and if our emotional brain takes any profit that moves we are never going to make it.

But the way in which our three brains interact with markets goes way beyond these fairly obvious examples.

Attacked by the market

However we trade, the market is, in one sense, continually probing our system and as it does this it will exploit any weakness. With fixed-odds bets we are relatively safe as we cannot let losses run in the same sense you can with a spread betting position. But this only affects one aspect of trading and there are many more.

Whilst the market probes the way we trade, it also probes us and our three brains.

The original work on the *triune* brain, as it is called, was done in the early 1970s by the American neurophysiologist Paul Maclean. It came to my attention through Tony Plummer's excellent book *Forecasting Financial Markets*. Tony's article *The Troubled Trader* is reproduced in that book and I felt it so important I also added it as an appendix to my own book *The Way to Trade*.

In the article Tony looks at how each of uses one of our brains as our *primary* and how the various ways in which we use our three brains tends to leave us open to different types of *attack* from the market. The scope of this short article does not allow me to look at this in detail but those of you who are already looking inside your own heads with new insight may well want to find out more about these three brains.

Others may prefer to hear no more about this subject.

But before you abandon consideration of your three brains it may be worthwhile to think about these everyday situations where the three brains can be seen to be trying to work together:

The three brains and everyday situation

Buying a new car – the thoughtful mind wants that economical practical little number, the emotional brain wants the Porsche! I find my thoughtful brain finally agrees with the emotional brain as it is cheaper to buy the car you want – that way you don't lose money when you decide to trade in the car your emotional brain didn't want after a few months. It is worth pointing out that we live our lives in our emotional brain – that is where we are happy and sad, proud and disappointed, angry and confident.

You see an attractive member of the opposite sex and go over to say hello. Your thoughtful self is clear; you just go and say "Hi" – what could be easier? Your emotional self ties itself up in knots of embarrassment and you end up doing nothing – possibly losing a lifetime's worth of loving contentment!

You find yourself in a difficult physical situation, maybe you are swimming and you find the tide is taking you further out. Your impulsive brain wants to swim as hard as possible for the shore but your thoughtful self thinks that to do this may wear you out and the tide seems to be taking you to one side where there is land closer. Your emotional brain is frightened and you try to control the panic.

> Successful trading is all about knowing yourself well and it is only when you understand how your three brains are going to react to different stimuli that you can make real progress.

It's all in your head

Before I conclude this chapter I must address another essential point. What we are trading is not the external object you may imagine, it is very much a product of our own brain, compounded by the fact we have three of them!

You may doubt this.

There is my share and my share price, there is my price screen, here is my system. What garbage is this? All these things are external and most definitely not inside my own brain – however many of them you say I have!

OK, bear with me; I believe I can establish this fact beyond all reasonable doubt.

The first point I will make is that there is so much information on the market that it is impossible to access and/or digest it all. If you were to try and digest it all you would need all the share prices of all the stocks, all the prices of all the futures and commodities, all the currency prices, plus all the technical indicators plus all the fundamental analysis. That alone is impossible, but added to that you would also need every traders' opinion and positions on the market to truly give you the full picture.

Clearly this is not possible and you are forced to focus on a small fraction of that information.

Who chooses this focus?

You and your three brains.

That is *strike one* – if you choose what information to look at then already this is becoming an internal matter, because that decision is liable to be subjective and may well have been produced by a random process.

Incidentally *focus* is a key concept and defines your trading approach and your success or failure.

Having chosen what we are going to look at what do we do with it?

This comes directly down to our three brains again. They decide what to do with information and a lot of this will be based on our experience. A lot of life is habit; habits that we have built up over many years. We have found that x works, so we continue to do x. Think about your day. How much of it is 100% habit. The way we dress, the way we eat, the people we talk to, the way we talk to them, the way we do our job, the way we run our business.

Just like a bell curve most of us have *survival* habits and we get on fine. We do not make the most of our opportunities but we get by and feed our children. A few develop *winning* habits and thrive. Another relatively small minority develop *losing* habits and end up in the gutter. I am not simply referring to financial matters here; losing habits can involve addiction and/or self destructive behaviour among many other things.

Then there are our results and the way in which our brains interact with the market, but I have already discussed that!

Finally, as I mentioned earlier, price can be summed up by this formula:

```
Price = Value x Sentiment
```

This is derived from the PE ratio which has long been used as a guide to value – I have just switched it around and I think it is more useful in this form in that it gives a clear indication of how prices are formed.

In this formula price is the actual price of a stock. Value is your benchmark of value – be it earnings, asset value, or whatever. Sentiment is the variable which is a measure of sentiment at that time. If you base *value* on earnings then *sentiment* becomes the PE ratio.

Chart 9.1: PE ratio

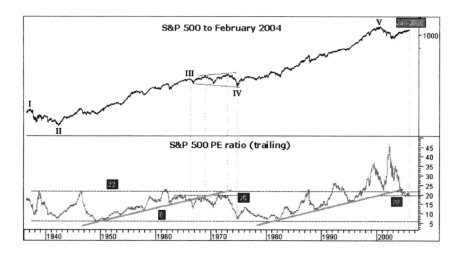

To make this discussion easier I will assume we measure value by earnings so that we can measure sentiment using the well-known PE ratio.

If we look at a long-term chart of the PE ratio, see above, we can see that the PE ratio on the S&P has been as low as 6-7 (1940s and 1980s) and as high as 47 (2000s). That is a variation of around 750% and the critical point to bear in mind is that this has a direct bearing on price. If *value* remains the same then that 750% variation is the amount of price movement caused solely by sentiment. To put this another way that 750% variation is in addition to any rise or fall in earnings during that period.

In this aspect it is clear the market is simply a maelstrom of human psychology. There is no logic to such a variation and I do not think we can escape the conclusion that the only reason we see such variation is because of human emotion and instinct. I do not wish to belabour the point but as markets go up they exert a strong urge to buy and as they go down they can cause *panic* selling. This effect of market action is one reason for such wide variation in sentiment.

Bear in mind that *sentiment* can turn on a dime whereas value requires a lot more work and effort. Is it any wonder we all have trouble working out where the market is going next?

Summary

In this chapter we have learnt:

- Human behaviour is even more complex than we thought
- We have three primary inputs into our behaviour – our *three* brains
- We do not trade externals – we trade ourselves
- Human psychology has a lot more to do with prices than *value*

10.

Statistics and Probability

If I am asked to name the one thing that a trader must have an awareness of it is…statistics!

I often say that most traders are fugitives from the law of averages and in this chapter I am going to explain why that is. As with most things in the trading environment this one is also multi-layered. Here are two layers to be getting on with:

- Statistically, **strings of losses** (and profits) will be much longer than you may think intuitively – meaning you will hit more losses in a row than you expect. I emphasise the losses here because it is the losses that can wipe you out. For some reason traders never seem too bothered about a run of profits – even though they rarely make the most of them.

- If you take a **risk which has a low probability** you should be fine the first time. But if you keep doing it – it will kill you! A real life example is drinking and driving. Cars are rarely stopped by the police in the UK and drink-drivers can get away with it. But keep doing it and you will be stopped, breathalysed and banned. Even worse you may kill someone. A corollary in the trading world is selling (aka writing) options.

Now I am going to look at both of these with particular regard to trading binary bets.

Strings of losses

When looking at strings of losses, binaries again have an advantage simply because you know exactly what is at risk. This is not the case with a spread bet – although guaranteed stops can make it so, at a cost. It is certainly not the case if you write options. This aspect is useful as it makes money management easier and more effective. Money management is what keeps you safe when things go wrong and maximises your profits when things go well. For example, you may decide to risk 2% per trade and that 2% be based on the balance in hand as it grows with profits and shrinks with losses. But in order to maximise your profit runs you increase to a risk of 3% after 2 profits.

Whole books have been written on money management; one particularly detailed work described something known as *optimal f* – a formula designed to keep you safe but give you the most bang for your buck in the good times. Unfortunately this concept proved difficult to master and gave rise to the trader's lament, "I've been optimally f'd!"

How long a string of losses should you expect?

Many traders have a hit rate around 50%; meaning around half their trades are profitable. Often the hit rate is a little less but that is fine as long as the average profit is in excess of the average loss – a good ratio is 2.5:1 (i.e. the average profit is 2.5 times the average loss).

> With a hit rate of 50% you can expect a string of 10 or 11 losers every 1000 trades. You can expect a string of 4 or 5 losers every 30 trades!.

That might surprise you, especially if you bear in mind that many traders abandon a system if it gives them 4 or 5 losers in a row – they consider it useless. But statistically you are bound to get 4 or 5 losers every 30 trades if your hit rate is 50%.

Don't believe me? Try tossing a coin 100 times and see what results you get.

Fugitives from the law of averages

The second point can be harder for traders to understand but it is even more critical. If your trading strategy has a flaw then, over time, the market will expose it. In this sense the market is a generator of random sequences and, over time, it will generate all possible sequences. This is why we see traders who do well consistently, suddenly hit a brick wall – the market has found the flaw in their approach! I should add that the flaw may not be in their trading system, it may be psychological. What, in the real world, we may call character can be a disaster for your trading.

It is precisely this process that I refer to when I say that many traders are fugitives from the law of averages. You can run, but you can't hide. You may be aware of the flaw in your approach, many traders are, but fail to admit it or address it.

The obvious strategy to illustrate this is writing options. When you write an option you become the bookie and bookies usually win but every now and then they take a big hit. So it is with writing options. Most months you do well, then BAM, you get hit for six. Human psychology is such that as the profits roll in initially the trader thinks he is a genius and he increases the amounts of money involved – thus when the hit comes it often wipes him out.

The flaw was that the trader had taken no account of sharp market action and had no hedge in place for this.

With binaries your risk is always strictly controlled and this sort of situation cannot arise, unless your money management system is utterly hopeless.

So when I say that most traders are fugitives from the law of averages this is what I mean. If you are not aware of how statistics affect your trading and if you do not fully understand how the market may impact on your trading approach, and on you personally, then it is simply a matter of time before the law (of averages) catches up with you.

Probability

Statistics leads into probability. It is by using statistics that you can compute probability.

Probability plays a central role in binary trading. Every binary price is an expression of the probability that the bet will prove true and win. Not exactly, of course, as you have to take into account the spread.

You must also bear in mind that the price is computed by an algorithm based on:

- **Price** – the price of the underlying market and in particular how it relates to this particular bet

- **Time** – in particular the time until expiry

- **Volatility** – an estimate of volatility over the life of the bet

- **Weight of money** – bet prices will tend to vary as more money gets on board

So the bet price reflects the probability as set out above; but what effect does, for example, an Elliott five have on this?

We see the market form a perfect five-wave rally and know to expect a pullback – a sell signal. This is not reflected in the calculation I have just mentioned and there is no way that it can be – it is simply an algorithm and cannot take account of the various buy and sell signals that all markets throw out on a fairly continuous basis.

But if you have traded for any period of time and if you have done any research into your trading approach you will know that it gives you an edge – if not, it needs some work.

Now I cannot quantify what effect your edge will have on the probabilities but if you know that the trading signal that you work with gives a 50% probability of a 30 point move in the direction of the signal then that will have a profound impact on how you view the price of the bet.

An example of how you may view bet pricing

Let's assume that FTSE is up 10 points and there are two hours left of that day's session. Your system gives you a buy signal and you find that the bet *FTSE to be up >30 points* is priced at 23/27 reflecting a 25% probability of FTSE closing up more than 30 points. However, your system has given a buy signal and you *know* that a fair price is around 50.

Of course you would not pay 50 as by doing that you would get no *value* on the deal. With no value you will not come out on top over numerous trades. But you don't have to pay 50, you can pay 27 – and based on the assumptions I have made you would lap that price up.

The important point here is how you might apply the edge you have to binary prices. If your system has any value then it should allow you to isolate good value bets.

We are now going to look at a more detailed example.

Here is a table showing how often the Dow stayed within the following ranges in a single day's session.

Table 10.1: Dow Index – range analysis

The Dow – Maximum move away from the prior close	Percentage of sessions within that range	Percentage of sessions between the two
<40 points	12.5%	-
<50 points	24.5%	12%
<60 points	35%	10.5%
<70 points	44%	9%
<80 points	55.5%	11.5%
<100 points	73.5%	18%
<120 points	85.5%	12.5%
<200 points	97%	11.5%

For example, 44% of all sessions the Dow closed with a change of less than 70 points from the previous close, and for 9% of all sessions the change was between 60 and 70 points.

This range analysis can be illustrated visually in the diagram below.[5]

Diagram 10.1: Dow Index daily changes (Jan 2007 – Aug 2008)

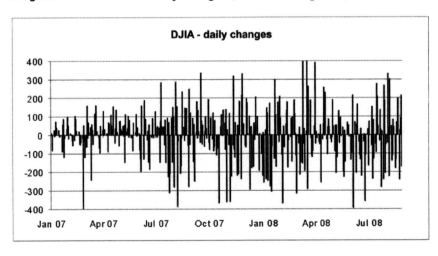

A simple look at the above diagram gives a feel for the range of daily changes of the DJIA.

---

[5] You can create such diagrams yourself by downloading the historic data from Yahoo and importing into Excel.

Here is the same data on FTSE:

Table 10.2: FTSE – range analysis

FTSE – Maximum move away from the prior close	Percentage of sessions within that range	Percentage of sessions between the two
<25 points	8.5%	-
<30 points	17%	8.5%
<35 points	29.5%	10.5%
<40 points	37.5%	8%
<45 points	50.5%	13%
<50 points	58%	7.5%
<60 points	74.5%	16.5%
<80 points	87.5%	13%

And, again, the range of daily changes can be illustrated visually:

Diagram 10.2: FTSE 100 Index daily changes (Jan 2007 – Aug 2008)

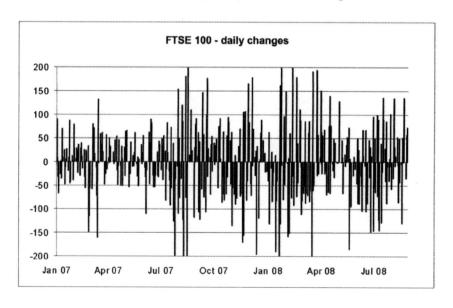

Before we start to use this data I need to make a few points:

1. This data was extracted from 200 trading sessions mainly from 2006.

2. The increased volatility in 2007/2008 would mean a more recent sample would produce different percentages.

3. All markets alternate between volatile times and non volatile times.

> If you decide you want to use data of this type you *must* do the research yourself so you are building on rock. To do otherwise would be to build on sand. Every successful trader I know does his/her own research – and plenty of it.

There are always assumptions built into any data such as this and also pitfalls – you need to know what they are.

Building a trading system

Let's say we want to build a trading system around the FTSE 50/50 Tunnel. The IG bet description is *FTSE to stay in the range +50/-50*.

We can go straight to the second table and see that FTSE stays in a +50/-50 range of the prior close 58% of the time. This means that we could pay 58 for this bet day in and day out and breakeven over time.

If we were to pay 50 rather than 58 we would win over time – a much better way to trade!

But what of large gap opens?

FTSE often opens well up or down and a number of these moves will take out the 50/50 Tunnel. Is this good or bad for our fledgling system?

It's good!

As long as our data is representative these big gap days are already in the data and it means that we could actually pay more than 58 for the bet and break even – the market is conveniently not allowing us to trade on a certain number of these bets which are sure losers – in fact actual losers at the open.

Note: If we were planning to sell these bets this factor would be a clear negative – eliminating trades which appeared profitable from the raw data.

It is relatively simple to do this sort of research in Excel (I can say this with confidence as I know virtually nothing about this program but still managed to use it for this purpose). Indeed I have just spent 15 minutes analysing the last 274 sessions of FTSE.

This gave a very different result – just 44 of those sessions stayed in the 50/50 range, that is just 16%!

With this sort of result you would not want to pay much more than 10 and you would have to get used to a larger proportion of losers and that can be psychologically draining.

Volatility and trends

In the example above volatility is clearly immensely important. Here is a list of some of the major variables which you may want to take into account when designing trading systems:

1. volatility

2. the trend

3. variation in bet pricing

4. news

To outline how you might deal with these variables in practice is beyond the scope of this book. It will depend enormously on the basics of your approach to the market and, as such, to deal with each factor properly would require a vast and very detailed manuscript – a separate book in fact.

To the majority of readers this would mean very little and those few who plan to develop systems which take into account these variables will, no doubt, develop their own unique techniques.

But I will say the following…

1. Volatility

There is a futures contract (traded on the CBOE) known as the VIX which is a measure of volatility in the US equity market. The price of this contract can give an indication of the market's view of the level of volatility.

Alternatively you can create your own calculation for volatility (there is no one correct method). For example, an average of the last x days' Hi-Lo ranges could be used. You might adopt a different pricing structure and different bets depending on what your volatility indicators were showing. Trading volatility extremes, both high and low, might be the basis of your entire system.

- If you are spread betting then you can expect bigger and faster moves. This is great for profit potential but means you may well have to allow wider stops and many traders are not happy to do this. In fact a trader can simply reduce position size, meaning less £s per point, and would end up risking the same amount with a wider stop,

- With binary bets and options, volatility can have a major effect on the prices and on the spread as the betting companies sometimes widen the spreads when it gets truly hairy – October 2008 is a good example.

- Widening spreads is *never* helpful as it makes both buying and selling more expensive, but the price skew which volatility creates can shift the balance of probabilities so that an alternative system becomes attractive.

- For example if you devise a system to *sell* binary Tunnel bets because prices are high you may decide to *buy* them if prices are skewed lower.

How is volatility measured?

There are various ways but the most common is to measure the rate of change over a specified period. This leads us to a key point: volatility is an historic measure – it measures the volatility that existed over the last x days, x hours, or x minutes.

This can make it useful and *Trading the News* [see Chapter 5] is an example of how this works:

- We place our bets when volatility is *low*, at that point we can *sell* Tunnels at high prices

- The news may create *high* volatility, possibly only for a very brief period

- This can push the price of the binary Tunnels *lower* giving us a good profit opportunity

- In fact this may also give us the opportunity to *buy* Tunnel bets at low prices. Especially if we believe the volatility is already over.

I am using Tunnel bets as an example here but similar strategies can be applied to other bets also. Having said that, Tunnels are a pure play on volatility as a move in either direction will send a Tunnel to zero.

It goes beyond the scope of this book to discuss the various formulae that can be used to measure volatility and, again, research into such matters can yield many advantages but it is something that you would need to do for yourself.

One simple approach to gauge volatility is to plot the difference in the highs and lows each day over a period (as illustrated in the following diagram).

Diagram 10.3: DJIA daily high-low range (Jan 2007 – Aug 2008)

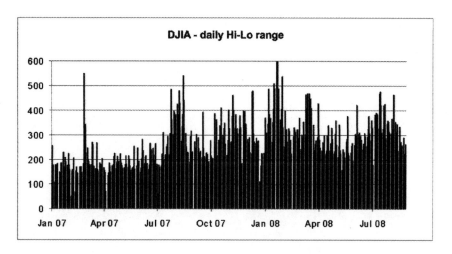

There are many, many ways in which to profit from markets and, in my experience, every successful trader ploughs his own furrow.

It is also true that for every way there is of making money there are at least ten ways of losing money and another ten traders who will take the wining approach and lose with it.

2. The trend

There are a vast number of ways in which to measure the trend, from the humble, but highly effective, trendline through Gann swing charts to various algorithms. The trend might be the basis of your entire system.

You may ask me what methods work and which don't. In my experience all methods *work* as well as any other but the intention here is not so much to get an edge from this part of the system but more to *define* the time frame in which you are interested. An edge is a bonus.

For example if you were to look at a monthly chart you may see that the market has been going steadily up for six months and conclude it is in an uptrend. But switch to the daily chart and you may see a clear downtrend. Look at an intraday chart, say a 10 minute bar, and the *trend* will be different again.

Successful traders learn to focus on one small aspect of market action and defining *your* trend is an important part of that.

3. Variation in bet pricing

I include this as a separate item even though it may be caused largely by volatility. But there can be other causes ranging from simple error, through price and volatility spikes, to weight of money. Looking for aberrant pricing might be the basis of your entire system.

By "variation in bet pricing" I mean the fact that prices will vary all the time. Volatility may be the simplest example of this. In times of low volatility the prices of OneTouches will tend to be *lower* as the market is going *slower* and will thus have less chance of touching the relevant level. In *faster* markets the OneTouch prices will tend to be *higher*.

In fact I did devise an entire system based on this concept and here is how I sent it out to my subscribers...

> Here is a trading system I have been working on for while and I made an excellent profit from it last night.
>
> It involves the Hi/Lo bets on the Dow. The two bets in question are:
>
> Wall Street cash high to be >+200; and Wall Street cash low to be <-200

With the high volatility at this time (October 2008) you can SELL these 2 bets and get in more than 100 – the maximum I have seen is around 120. This may seem like a bonanza but bear in mind you are selling two bets and the Dow has recently seen both a high in excess of +200 and low beyond -200 – meaning both bets might go to 100.

I will give you an example. You sell both bets and get in 75 for one and 25 for the other. A total of 100 (75 + 25 = 100) at £10 per point = £1000.

The Dow moves above +200 and then below -200 sending each bet to 100 and you are down £1000!

That is not the idea of the system and to avoid this we will close the other leg if the Dow takes out one leg. So if the Dow goes to >+200 the bet "Wall Street cash high to be >+200" will go to 100 and we will then close "Wall Street cash low to be <-200" and this may cost around 20.

If so our loss would be £200 (+100-100-20 = -20 x £10 = £200).

How often does the Dow take out both extremes?

This is something that you need to research yourself. If you want to use this system you need to become an expert in how it works and if I give you such information you will never be an expert.

I would suggest opening your positions when the Dow has around 2 hours left to trade. Normally this would be around 7pm, but this week it is around 6pm.

Once positioned you now look to sell the bet "Wall Street to keep in the range -200 to +200" at 50 or more.

It is this third bet that locks in your profit. Last night I sold the Hi/Los for a total of 100 each and then sold the 200/200 Tunnels for between 50 and 80.

It worked out like this…

Sold Hi/Los for 100 at £10 pp = +£1000

Sold Tunnels at 65 (av.) at £20 pp = +£1300

The Dow went to +200 and this cost me £1000 for the Hi bet but I got to keep the £1300 from the Tunnels which went to zero at that point.

I then closed the Lo bet at 15 at £10 pp = -£150.

Total net profit = £1150 (+£1000 – £1000 + £1300 – £150 = £1150)

The logic here is that the risk on the Tunnel bets was £700 as I would have lost if they went to 100. The average risk was 35 (100 – 65 = 35) at £20 pp = £700.

But that risk would only occur if the Dow stayed in the range -200 to +200 and if it did I would get to keep the £1000 from selling the Hi/Lo bets so I would still win £300.

The key risk is that the Dow would take out the range before I had the chance to sell the Tunnel bets and then I would have expected to lose around £200.

This system should also work on FTSE in the -100 to +100 range but I have not researched that as fully.

Take it slowly to start with and use small sums until you are confident in how it works.

As the volatility has reduced the Hi/Lo prices have also reduced and, as I write in November 2008, you cannot get 100+ for the two Hi/Lo bets. But volatility will be back and so this system may again prove very useful.

However there is one open point – did this opportunity come about because of the volatility or was there also an element of IG misquoting these bets? At this point I don't know the answer to that question and I don't really need to. I bagged a good profit and, if I see the opportunity again, I will do it again.

4. News

Chapter 5 outlines a trading system based entirely on the news and this is another factor you may want to incorporate in your system. However, as previously discussed, binaries do give you distinct advantages when news comes out. Spread betters may prefer to enter *after* the news comes out if they feel they are then offered very attractive prices.

Summary

In this chapter we have learnt:

- Every trader needs a basic working knowledge of statistics
- Probability goes to the core of binary betting
- Four key variables which we may want to take into account in our trading

11.

Developing a Trading System

In the previous three chapters I have given you a number of ideas of how you might trade the binaries; and in the Appendix I give you a specific aim and a plan for increasing the size of your trading as you make profits.

In this chapter I am going to set out in clear steps how you should go about testing your approach both on paper and for real.

How do you maximise your profits?

The process is to progressively increase your trading as you make profits but always keep a tight control on risk.

Trading ideas

The first step is the trading idea and by this I mean the basic plan underlying your trading. For example it might involve a particular chart pattern, an algorithm based on early action, or a combination of moving averages.

Let me give you an example of a trading idea.

Example 11.1: A trading idea

You notice that *every* time FTSE pokes its head beyond a round number, like 5000, 4500, or 4700, it always turns tail and heads back in the opposite direction.

You think:

> *Hmm, this looks interesting; I must be able to make some money out of this,*

You determine to do just that and it is when you make that decision that the *trading idea* starts to become the *trading system*.

This chapter sets out a methodical and disciplined way in which to create your system from your idea. But I want to take this example a little further and illustrate how most traders do it.

The next day you see FTSE move up and break above 5000 – you pile in to sell the market.

FTSE keeps going up and you finally close your position with a loss in excess of 100 points at £10 per point. You are down over a grand!

But you have learnt quite a lot:

- You have learnt that FTSE does not reverse *every* time it breaks beyond a round number.

- The idea of risk control may start making an impression.

- You may have learnt that this is far too risky and that you are going back to bungee jumping.

- Alternatively you may have learnt that you need to approach this in a far more methodical and disciplined fashion [now, where's John Piper's latest book when I need it!]

Of course you might win on your first trade – beginners are very much focused on profits and this triggers the Law of Attraction which means they often get them.

If you do win then it will reinforce your beliefs, which are erroneous, and you may not learn very much until the market finally cleans you out.

Far better to systemise the idea now and start the testing process.

To systemise your idea of trading whenever FTSE moves beyond a round number you have various options and here are a few:

- You could wait for a 20 point penetration and then trade at that point with your stop 20 points beyond your entry level. In the situation above where FTSE rallies above 5000, this approach would mean you sell at 5020 with your stop at 5040.

- You could wait for the penetration to reverse, trade the market after FTSE has already retraced its steps and then place your stop beyond the extreme. In the situation above, where FTSE rallies above 5000, this approach would mean you sell at, say, 4995 with your stop at 5035 if the high FTSE made was at 5030.

- You could place a limit order to trade at the round number and a stop to take you out if you are down x points. In the situation above where FTSE rallies above 5000, this approach would mean you sell at 5000 with your stop at 5000 + x.

All of these approaches have pros and cons – here are a few:

- The first would mean you would miss trades where the penetration is less than 20 points.
- The second will catch all the signals where there is a reversal but you may have a very wide stop.
- The third would mean you will get stopped out from time to time from trades that would have been profitable.

Incidentally this trading idea is based on an approach I call a *failed break* [and which is explained in detail in my book *The Way To Trade.*]

Ten plus three trading ideas

The concept of a *trading idea* is an important one and I set out below 10 further ideas that you may find have some merit:

- Buying or selling a breakout from the range seen in the first hour of trading
- Trading away from double bottoms or tops
- Trading the News [see Chapter 5]
- Looking for Elliott threes – the fastest moves in the sequence [see Chapter 6]
- Moving average crossovers
- An idea based on the time of day, for example sell binary Tunnels after midday at 80+
- Buy a particular binary if the bet reaches a set price [this idea is detailed later in this chapter]
- Use a combination of technical indicators, for example stochastics and MACD
- Use chart patterns such as triangles and head and shoulders
- Trading the trend using NoTouches [see Chapter 4]

I also set out three further ideas from *The Stock Market Almanac 2008*. I am including these for two reasons, first because I think they have merit; and second because I want to make the point that there are plenty of sources of trading ideas of which the *Almanac* is one:

- The tables on pages 28 and 32 (of the Almanac) provide the expectation of how long a string of profits or losses will continue and this expectation could mean money in the bank with the right trading idea.
- The Friday-Monday strategy outlined on page 54 is another idea that may conceal hidden gold.
- The Winter v Summer portfolio concept on pages 96 and 98 is another which might provide ample food for thought.

I have expanded this section somewhat beyond binary bets and these ideas are meant as general trading ideas but many will also have binary applications. Some of the above are ideas I have not had time to work on yet. Put in the research and you may beat me to it!

Trading systems

For the remainder of this chapter I am assuming that you have the idea and that you have done some initial testing on it. To do this you will need to convert the *trading idea* into a fairly mechanical *trading system*.

The process is best started with the idea which has the most promise and this idea also needs to be fairly mechanical so that it is not affected by any mood swings you may have. Traders without a mechanical approach find that they are prone to trade on the basis of their emotions at any time. Experienced traders will have overcome such problems, although not necessarily completely.

It is also important that the idea is fairly simple as you need to develop your trading skills and you won't want to cut your teeth on a monstrous trading concept which may well finish you off before you start.

The goal is to start small and then to increase your trading size in two, possibly three, key ways:

1. The amount you trade on each position.
2. The number of markets you trade.
3. You may also want to increase the frequency with which you trade each market, though your system may not allow this.

The metrics

You must be able to measure your system's *metrics*.

Knowing the percentage of winning trades you make and the ratio of the average amount you make to the average amount you lose is an extremely important part of this process.

Here are the two main trading system metrics explained in more detail:

1. **The number of winners divided by the total number of trades (Metric ONE)**
   Very often this works out at slightly less than 50%, maybe 45% – depending on the type of system you use. You can achieve much higher success rates but this tends to have an adverse effect on the second metric.

2. **The average of your profits divided by the average of your losses (Metric TWO)**
   This measures your total gains from your winning trades and divides them by the number of those trades. It then measures the total losses from your losing trades and divides that figure by the number of those trades. The ratio is then the first divided by the second and it needs to be in excess of 2, preferably in excess of 2.5.

Example 11.2: Metrics in action

We may take our first 100 trades.

1. First metric: If 40 are winners and 60 are losers; our first metric is 40%.

2. Second metric: Our 40 winners make £20,000, making the average of our winning trades £500 per trade. Our 60 losers lose £10,000, making the average of our losing trades £167 per trade. The second metric is 3 (£500 divided by £167) – which is excellent!

Why is it excellent?

Because our profit is £10,000 on 100 trades. So, even though a majority of our trades lost money (six out of every ten in fact), we still made money overall, because our win/loss ratio (the second metric) was very high.

Why are the metrics so important?

Because every trading system is unique, as is every trade, and your system will work differently on every market you trade. These figures are more than numbers; they are the benchmarks you need to reach before you can expand your trading.

If you see a problem as you develop this, you can immediately see what it is by comparing your results to your benchmarks.

Developing the system

Two requirements

1. I have already mentioned that you will need to develop your own trading idea and there is plenty of help available in this book.

2. You will also need to have undertaken some initial testing on paper to see how the system might operate in the market itself. This is not a complex process and follows naturally from the initial design of the system.

Now it is time to start

As you test the validity of a new trading system, it's very important to spend ample time on the first few steps, especially paper trading. It is all free at that point – if you don't put in the groundwork you may find that you blow your entire budget trading a system which has not been properly tested.

Each step has been carefully positioned in terms of least risk and least cost. It is how you should approach everything in life – go for the low hanging fruit first, make sure the system works, and then maximise your efforts.

Step one – Back-test your idea

The first step is back-testing. Nice and simple with no real money at risk. This is the key stage but many people can't be bothered.

Why not?

Because they want to trade, they want to have fun, not work at it.

Don't make this mistake. Back-testing is the foundation on which everything else is built. It is also the stage during which you get to see how your system parameters work in the real world.

One recommendation I would make is to visualise that you are actually doing the trades and the bets as you work through this. That way you will begin to understand how it will feel when your money is at risk as the market (or the match) bounces up or down until you end up with your final profit or loss.

At this stage you can also change some of your parameters to enhance system performance. The best systems are stable, meaning that minor changes in a parameter will not have a huge effect on profitability. If minor changes have huge effects then that is not a good sign.

Example 11.3: Back-testing an idea

To make this process real for you I am going to put forward an idea and go through each of the six stages.

- **The idea**
  Buy either the bet *FTSE to be up at 12pm* or the bet *FTSE to be down at 12pm* if the price goes to 12 or lower. Allow the bet to expire at either zero or 100.

- **The reasoning**
  This system seeks to make money out of the early action on FTSE. If you examine how FTSE behaves in the first hour of trading you will see it can be fairly erratic and early losses or gains can be reversed. This is the sort of action this idea is looking for.

This is a simple example of a trading system. It defines the entry (when the bet price is 12 or lower) and the exit (allow to expire at zero or 100). That is all you need although systems can be a lot more complex.

Can we make money with this idea?

We are doing this process to find out.

Table 11.1: Back-testing results

Date	Possible entry	My entry	Possible exit	My exit	Possible result
10-Aug	<10		0		0 -10
11-Aug	<10		>90		E +82
14-Aug	<10		0		0 -10
15-Aug	<10		0		0 -10
16-Aug	<10		0		0 -10
17-Aug	<10		87		D +77
18-Aug	<10		0		0 -10
21-Aug	11		100		E +89
22-Aug	10		100		E +90

This table needs some explanation, these are the columns:

Date

There are only 9 entries because it is difficult to get access to binary prices going back further. You could use the underlying market with pre-set parameters or apply a binary formula but I prefer to extend the paper trading period to compensate for the shorter back-testing period.

Possible Entry

The possible entry is either given a value of 10 or more or is stated as <10 meaning *"less than 10."*

Possible Exit

This sets out the best possible exit point of the bet. If a value of 0 is stated it means the bet simply moved down to 0 with no profit opportunity. A price above 0 identifies the best possible exit giving maximum profit although this does not imply the system captured all of that potential.

My Entry/My Exit

There are no entries for "my entry" or "my exit" as we are not taking trades at this point but these columns will become useful as we move onto later stages of the process.

Possible result

I categorised the results as follows:

0 – a loss of the amount risked

A – a profit of less than 20

B – a profit of 20-40

C – a profit of 40-60

D – a profit of 60-80

E – a profit in excess of 80

I use an Excel spreadsheet to track the results but this is not essential.

Nine trades is not a large sample and is not even statistically relevant (meaning we cannot rely on the results). Nevertheless, it is useful for illustrative purposes and we can be encouraged by the results which can be summarised as:

Metric #1

Four profits out of nine trades – **44.4%**.

Metric #2

Average loss was 10 points as all the losses were 10 points.

There were 4 profits. Two went all the way and the bets closed at 100. The other two gave maximum potential at 77 and 82. This raises the question *do we take profits early*, say at 80 (giving a profit of 70 after the entry at 10) or do we let these run all the way? If we run all the way we end up with only two profits as the other two will close at zero. If we close at 80 we will get all four profits but those which had given us around 90 points of profit will only give us 70 points.

This sort of decision goes to the heart of system design.

If we decide to close at 80 we end up with 4 profits of around 70, average profit 70 and metric #2 becomes **7** (70 divided by 10).

Multiplying the two metrics together gives us 311% which is great but, don't forget, it is also unreliable with so few trades.

Here are the results set out in the form of a table.

Table 11.2: Metrics analysis for test trading idea

Betting concept	Buy FTSE to be up/down by 12:00 if priced at 12 or less
Total trades	9
Number of profitable trades	4
Number of losing trades	5
Metric #1 – % of winning trades	44.44% (4 divided by 9)
Average profit from winning trades	70 (based on exiting at 80)
Average loss from losing trades	10
Metric #2 – average profit divided by average loss	7
Metric #1 x Metric #2	311% (44.44% x 7)

Having completed step one it is now time to move on to paper trading.

Step two – Paper-trade your idea

Up to this point you have done everything you can do to test your system. With the results produced from back-testing you can calculate your metrics, as in the examples above, and once your system shows the right metrics this means that you have an edge. In general as long as metric #1 multiplied by metric #2 produces at least 120% you have a reasonable edge.

If we look again at the metrics in the example at the beginning of this chapter we see that Metric #1 was 40% and Metric #2 was 3. Multiply these together (40% times 3) gives us 120%. Anything less than 50% is loss-making. Anything less than 75% is vulnerable to become loss-making.

It is time for step two.

No, you do not rush out and throw thousands at the markets; step two still involves no money.

There are a number of reasons for this.

One is that in the development stage there is a pitfall called *over-optimisation* which means that you may have *curve-fitted* your system to the market data you are working on – for example if there is one extraordinary move and you design your system just to catch that your idea is unlikely to work at other times and on other markets.

Another reason is simply that the data you use may be atypical.

In fact there are lots of reasons and paper trading is a positive in itself because you get another chance to visualise that you are trading for real and this time it is real-time. You cannot push fast forward and must wait for the market moves to unravel. As the market gyrates around pushing you into profit or loss you may find that this has an emotional affect on you. This will give you a feel for how it feels to place bets for real.

Example 11.4: Paper-trading an idea

This example follows on from the previous example in step one. I have not included all of the paper trades in the table below as my aim is to show you how this is done, not to repeat a large number of trades which will merely fill up pages for no particularly good reason. If you like the idea behind this example then you will learn a lot more if you test it out for yourself following these guidelines.

Table 11.3: Paper-trading results

Date	Possible entry	My entry	Possible exit	My exit	Possible result
1-Sep	<10		<24		A +14
4-Sep	<10		0		0 -10
5-Sep	not to 10 before 10 – no trade				
6-Sep	<10		0		0 -10
7-Sep	<10		0		0 -10
8-Sep	<10		25		A +15
11-Sep	<10		0		0-10
12-Sep	<10		100		E +90
13-Sep	<10		>60		C+50
14-Sep	<10		>55		C+45
15-Sep	11		100		E+89
18-Sep	no trade		-		
19-Sep	<10		0		0-10
20-Sep	no trade		-		
21-Sep	15		100		E+85

Some notes on the table above

- As I said these are just a sample of the paper-trading results, not all of them.

- Also I have now introduced a new rule which is that we want to see the price at 12 or less by 10:00 am (GMT). This is logical as price will tend to get nearer extremes as expiry looms and I found this rule eliminated some of the losses from the back-testing phase.

- If you introduce a new rule at this stage you will need to go back and revise the results to date. You may well eliminate losing trades, but do you also eliminate winning trades?

- On 21 September I entered at 15 because of *other* favourable factors. It is your choice whether to allow such flexibility when testing out your own ideas.

Here are the results.

Table 11.4: Summary results

Betting concept	Buy *FTSE to be up/down* by 12pm if priced at 12 or less before 10am
Total trades	40 (always aim for at least this number)
Number of profitable trades	12
Number of losing trades	28
Metric #1 – % of winning trades	30% (12 divided by 40)
Average profit from winning trades	68 (based on exiting at 80)
Average loss from losing trades	11
Metric #2 – average profit divided by average loss	6.2
Metric #1 x Metric #2	186% (30% x 6.2)- still excellent but a lot lower

At this point we have both back-tested and paper-traded our idea and produced 40 results, which is becoming statistically relevant. It is still a small sample but we can now feel more confident that our idea has validity – that it does give us an edge.

Two important points:

1. Note how the system performance has deteriorated as the sample becomes bigger. This was always likely as the initial results were almost too good to be true.

2. As we test the system we will start to think about how to make it better, such as restricting trades to before 10:00 am which gives the bet more time to come good.

Step three – risk

As a trader there are two factors which you will become very familiar with, at least you will if you are going to succeed. These two factors are:

1. money management

2. risk control.

The first concerns how much you risk on each position and when you increase or reduce that amount. The second is more general and simply means reducing and controlling risk at all times. The markets are very high risk; to win you must adopt a very low risk approach.

I wanted to mention this before we get on to real trading as controlling your risk is the single most important factor that will help you win. Not controlling your risk is a short cut to the poor house! Thankfully, if you trade binary bets in the ways I suggest risk control is built-in.

If you decide to adopt the markets as your road to riches then you are going to need to study these concepts. If you are betting for fun then they are still useful concepts which may well enhance your pleasure. I will say no more about these two key factors right now as we will be looking at these in more detail in a later chapter.

Step four – you trade for real (but use small sums to do so)

We are now leaving our safe environment and hitting the markets for real. However, we want to keep our risk to a minimum and so here are three suggestions:

1. Keep your bet size to a minimum until you start to make money.

2. Some of the spread betting companies let you trade for as little as 1p per point for an initial period, some for longer periods – do that. In fact you might choose to do step 2 in this way.

3. Just trade one market to start with – choose the market that tested best.

Trading with real money will affect you in unexpected ways. It will trigger emotional and instinctive responses that may make you break your trading rules. This is important as you have just spent a fair amount of time building your system which means you have just developed those rules.

There are three points here:

1. The more visualisation you did in steps one and two the better you will be able to deal with trading for real.

2. Even if you notice that you are breaking your rules you may not be able to stop yourself the first time – especially if it gives you a better profit. But try harder the next time.

3. If you feel that a change to your rules is a good idea then simply repeat steps one and two and re-test!

Example 11.5: Real time trading

This example follows on from the earlier examples in this chapter. I have not included all of the trades in the table below for the reasons set out in those earlier examples.

Table 11.5: Real trading results

Date	Possible entry	My entry	Possible exit	My exit	Possible result	My result
26-Sep	<10	13	0	0	0-10	-13
27-Sep	<10	13	0	0	0-10	-13
28-Sep	<10	13	0	0	0-10	-13
29-Sep	<10	13	100	70	E+90	+57
2-Oct	<10	13	0	0	0-10	-13
3-Oct	<10	-	87	-	D+77	-
4-Oct	12	13	100	100	E+88	+87
5-Oct	No trade					
6-Oct	<10	13	0	0	-10	-13
9-Oct	13	13	0	52	-13	+49
10-Oct	<10	13	0	0	-10	-13

I have made this extract realistic in that when it came to trading the system I did not follow the rules and my trades diverged. In particular:

- I decided to enter at 13 or better

- On 29 September I got out early, not waiting for 80.

- On 3 October I missed the trade and it was, of course, a winner.

- On 9 October I again got out early at 52 but did better than the system.

I was in two minds as to whether to show this divergence as there is an implication that it is all right. This is not the case but it may be inevitable. But note that the system beat me hands down which is what normally happens.

Here are the system results set out in the form of a table.

Table 11.6: Summary results for the system

Betting Concept	Buy *FTSE to be up/down by 12pm* if priced at 12 or less before 10am
Total trades	40 (always aim for at least this number)
Number of profitable trades	13
Number of losing trades	27
Metric #1 – % of winning trades	32.5% (13 divided by 40)
Average profit from winning trades	68 (based on exiting at 80)
Average loss from losing trades	11
Metric #2 – average profit divided by average loss	6.2
Metric #1 x Metric #2	202% (32.5% x 6.2)

Here are "my trading" results.

Table 11.7: Summary results for my trading

Betting System Used	Buy *FTSE to be up/down by 12pm* if priced at 13 or less before 10am
Total trades	37 (3 missed)
Number of profitable trades	11 (winning trades tend to be faster so are easier to miss)
Number of losing trades	26
Metric #1 – % of winning trades	29.9% (11 divided by 37)
Average profit from winning trades	54 (because of early exits)
Average loss from losing trades	13
Metric #2 – average profit divided by average loss	4.2
Metric #1 x Metric #2	126% (29.9% x 4.2) – still positive

Step four is only over when you are making consistent profits – do not even think about going on to step five until this is the case.

Step five – increase your trading size

This is a major step forward. I have known many traders who only now start to trade the amounts they had intended to trade at step one. I have also known many traders who have simply skipped steps one to four and all of these have failed.

The silly thing is that there is no point in skipping steps one to four as all you could possibly lose by doing those steps is some time. What you lose by not doing those steps is any chance of success.

Think about it.

Step five is fundamental for another reason. Up to this point we have been focused on losses, on what our trading might cost us. Now we are focused on profits.

If we had adopted step five as our first step we would also have been focused on profits but we would have been living in a fool's paradise.

We would have known nothing about the markets and have had no useful data (our metrics) on our trading idea. But as we have reached step five we have fully tested our idea.

We *know we are going to win before we start*!

This is not to say it is going to be easy. There will be setbacks along the way. You may find that your system suffers from practical problems you were not aware of when you started. But everything worthwhile in life suffers from such problems and you are building on rock, not sand. As you move forwards all the work you have put in already will stand you in good stead for the future.

You may find that you have to go back and modify your system; re-test the parameters. No problem! You have done it once, it will be a lot easier the second time.

Step six – Further increase trading size as profits grow and start to trade other markets

You're on a roll!

You've worked on your idea and proven that it works on paper. Then you went into the real world and it worked there too. So you increased position size and the money is rolling in.

The next step is another major advance in that you again increase position size, and start to trade other markets – but only after carefully testing (i.e. going through steps one to four on that market if you have not already done so).

At this stage I would also strongly recommend developing other trading strategies. Markets do change and the more profitable systems you have, the better prepared you will be in case of adverse changes.

Conclusion

The six step process is not hard and you may find it more challenging to discover a trading system which you can profitably take through these steps.

But the more work you put in the more experience you will get.

If you persevere you will get there.

Addendum: Lessons from The Black Swan

I spent a few days skiing in Andorra recently and I took Nassim Taleb's latest book, *The Black Swan*, with me.

It is an excellent book. But for some reason it prompted me to realise something that has been a bit of a question up until now:

Why do so many traders with successful systems still manage to lose money?

It is quite a problem – everything is in place but the profits do not roll.

Example 11.6: A typical system

If we look at an example I think we can get an insight into the reasons for this. It is fairly typical that a good system will produce around 50% of winners – it can do this as the average profit is greater than the average loss. So, let's assume the average loss is £200 and let's further assume that 40% of the trades are winners but only modestly and they make £200 as well. The remaining 10% are the trades that bring home the bacon. Let's say they average a £750 profit.

So if we do 100 trades we have 50 losers at £200 each making a total loss of £10,000. We then have 40 winners at £200 making a profit of £8000 plus 10 other winners bringing in £7500. Over 100 trades the net result is a gain of £5500 (£8000 + £7500 – £10,000 = £5500).

That is money you can take to the bank. The figures I quote above are assumed to be net of any commissions payable. Here is a table showing the same thing.

Table 11.8: Summary results for this system

Trades	Results
Total trades	100
Number of profitable trades	50
Number of losing trades	50
Metric #1 – % of winning trades	50% (50 divided by 100)
Average profit from "small" winners	£200
Total profit from "small" winners	£8000 (£200 x 40)
Average loss from losing trades	£200
Total loss from losing trades	£10,000 (£200 x 50)
Net loss from "small wins" less losers	£2000 (£8000 – £10,000)
Average profit from "big" winners	£750
Total profit from "big" winners	£7500 (£750 x 10)
Overall net profit	£5500 (£8000 + £7500 – £10,000)
Average profit from both "big" and "small" winners	£310 (£8000 + £7500 divided by 50)
Metric #2 – average profit divided by average loss	1.55
Metric #1 x Metric #2	77.5% (50% x 1.55) – tight

So what goes wrong?

I think the main problem is simply that the better trades can be hard to catch. If the market ploughs through the entry point with speed and if we are slightly slow (or late) we may suddenly find that our 10 or 20 point risk tolerance is no longer enough to get on board. Our response may be to say, "Oh well, there are plenty more opportunities." But this response is not good enough. There may be plenty more opportunities but the good trades we cannot miss – they are what make the difference between overall profit and loss. Miss those trades and you may as well give up now. It is like going to the office but then skipping the days when they hand out the monthly salary cheque.

Also bear in mind that some of the less profitable trades may be pretty fast at the point of entry so you may well miss some of those as well. That is not so bad but bear in mind that you will *never* miss a losing trade – Oh No – they will always give you an easy entry point because they are going to go the wrong way.

If we look at these factors:

- missing a good proportion of the best trades,
- missing a few of the less profitable trades,
- catching all the losers

If we then add in human emotions, which will tend to make us exit the best trades too early, we are forced to conclude: is it any wonder we are all too prone to turn a winning system into a loser?

This may all seem very negative and we have not even touched on the fact that we tend to ignore our system a lot of the time. But the fact is when we know where we are going wrong we stand a much better chance of getting it right next time! So, for me, this is a potentially very positive message!

Summary

The material in this chapter will be of particular interest to those who wish to take a serious approach to binary bets. We look at a six-step process which starts with a betting idea and ends with a fully systemised approach which has been carefully tested and is giving us profits.

To make the process clearer I have given examples at Steps 1, 2 and 4 showing the sort of results you may get from your testing and the divergences which tend to appear once you start to trade your idea for real.

12.

System Testing

In this chapter I am going to take the idea of system testing a little further and give you a method to generate trading results without actually doing the trading. A fairly neat trick but one that should prove extremely useful.

I often work with other traders and one of the aspects I most enjoy is the interchange of ideas. Any good idea that improves our performance just one jot is going to reward us many times over.

I often speak to traders who tell me that they are so close to success. Others tell me that they have lost £10,000, £20,000 and sometimes a lot more. But the space between huge success and failure can be very small in this business. You only need a small edge to bridge that gap.

What might one good idea be worth to those who are already so close?

I would suggest many thousands of pounds!

I believe this is just such an idea and all you need are 100 or so marbles – 30p each from Hamleys!

The Marble Game

First you need to keep a record of your trades

This idea comes from Van Tharp, a leading trading psychologist in the US.

It is a simple idea, but effective. You need a record of your trades, and initially this may present some of you with a major stumbling block. It has always been my position that many traders enter the markets not primarily to make money but for other reasons, such as:

- for fun
- for the challenge involved
- to bolster prestige or self-esteem
- other emotional reasons.

Such traders tend not to treat trading as a business and records can be somewhat thin on the ground. Of course, there will be brokerage/spread betting statements, but going through all those to produce a record of your trading may seem too much like work. To the business trader, work is what is expected, but others may not feel the same way.

I will continue to explain how this works and then you can decide whether the work involved makes sense.

Now split your trades into groups

Once you have a list of all your trades you need to decide how these should be grouped by profit. Tharp suggests a concept he calls "minimum loss", but a more familiar term may be "lowest common denominator." This means you look for a low number and then you group all your trades into multiples of that number.

You do not want too many different groups and if your profits vary between £100-£2000 and your losses between £250-£1000 you may settle on £250 as your base unit.

You would then ignore all trades which win or lose less than, say, £150 and round all other trades up or down to the following groups.

To complete the picture I have added different marbles to each group and I will explain how this works below:

Table 12.1: Your trades classified in groups

Profit/loss	Groups	Marble	Number of trades in each group
Profit of £250	1:1	White	10
Profit of £500	2:1	Yellow	7
Profit of £750	3:1	Green	4
Profit of £1000	4:1	Brown	8
Profit of £1250	5:1	Silver	5
Profit of £1500	6:1	Gold	2
Profit of £1750	7:1	Eyeball	3
Profit of £2000	8:1	Leopard skin	3
Loss of £250	-1:1	Red	31
Loss of £500	-2:1	Orange	20
Loss of £750	-3:1	Turquoise	3
Loss of £1000	-4:1	Skull	2
Loss of £1250	-5:1	Purple	0
Loss of £1500	-6:1	Terra Cotta	1
Loss of £1750	-7:1	Spots	0
Loss of £2000	-8:1	Stripes	1

As in the table above you may find that some of these groups (for example losses of £1250, purple marbles) do not have any trades in them and I should mention at this point that you need a statistically relevant number of trades. Meaning at least 40 but preferably 100. There are 100 trades in the table above, being 36 winners and 54 losers.

Exercise: Apply the calculations outlined in Chapter 9 and work out the metrics of this system.

Would you trade it?

The next step is to buy your "hardware"

Once you have populated these groups with your trades, you then need to count up the number of active groups. Each group is to be represented by a different coloured marble and you will need to go out and buy these marbles.

You need one marble for each trade and every trade in the same group has the same sort of marble. So you may decide that the group of 8:1 losses gets a black marble and if you have 1 trade in that group, as in the table above, you need 1 black marble. If you have 100 trades then you will need 100 marbles. Every group will have a marble with different colours and/or patterns and they need to be easily distinguishable.

Once you have sorted your trades into the appropriate groups and acquired your marbles you are ready to begin. I should add that each marble merely represents a trading result, although you will have to acquire your marbles in some way you are merely acquiring a token representing different trading results.

But first a word about theory...

What you have done up to this point is modelled your trading results. You have ignored any hopes and aspirations you may have as regards your trading and simply listed your results. In this respect you have chosen the results you want to list. For example, you have decided how far back to go. You may only have taken trades of one particular type, or on one particular market. The essential point is that you have taken trades you have actually done with all the imperfections that implies.

Having said all that you could use this process based on your paper trading results – it might well prove as useful.

Setting the rules

To start playing the game you now have to decide two additional factors:

1. The amount of capital you are trading – I would suggest £10,000 or £100,000, which keeps the mathematics a little simpler.

2. Your money management system – you might go for a risk of 2% on each trade based on the capital left after the previous trade.

Off you go!

You then put all the marbles into an opaque bag and start to trade.

You do this by picking out one marble at a time and then recording your trading result. So if the first marble is green, a 3:1 profit, and you are risking 2% (which is £200 of £10,000) then you first result is a profit of £600.

Your capital becomes £10,600 and you risk £212 on the next trade – 2% of £10,600. You then do 100 trades computing your results as you go.

Critically make sure you replace each marble in the bag once it has been traded! Each time you trade the full range of options are open to the market and if you do not replace the marbles that will no longer be the case.

Here is a table setting out a set of typical results you might get based on the groupings in the table above. I have set out 10 trades in the following table but I would suggest you do at least 100.

Table 12.2: The Marble Game – results

Starting capital	Risk 2% on each trade	Marble	Profit/loss	Closing capital
£10,000	£200 (2% of £10,000)	Silver – Profit of 5:1	+£1000 (£200 x 5)	£11,000 (£10,000 + £1000)
£11,000	£220	Orange – Loss of 2:1	-£440	£10,560
£10,560	£211	Skull – Loss 4:1	-£844	£9716
£9716	£194	Leopard skin – Profit of 8:1	+£1552	£11,268
£11,268	£225	Yellow – Profit 2:1	+£450	£11,718
£11,718	£234	Orange – Loss of 2:1	-£468	£11,250
£11,250	£225	Red – Loss of 1:1	-£225	£11,025
£11,025	£220	Silver – Profit of 5:1	+£1100	£12,125
£12,125	£242	Red – Loss of 1:1	-£242	£11,883
£11,883	£237	Green – Profit of 3:1	+£711	£12,594

Note: Van Tharp does sell software so that you can play this game on your computer and also offers a limited version as a free trial. However there is value in working though this more slowly and visualising the trades and your emotions as the results come through. Although the software allows you to play the game you still have to work out the groupings of your trades and then input these groupings into the software.

The lessons you might learn

Here is what you can learn by doing this:

1. You replicate possible future trading results and you do this with extreme accuracy if your trading results and groupings are themselves accurate.

2. You check that your money management rules make sense – in particular you will see how high are your chances of being wiped out.

3. If you visualise each trading result as being real you experience some of the emotions as if from the actual trading.

4. You can think about the sequences that are generated and possibly formulate new trading rules that will improve your results.

5. Within an hour or so you may replicate many months of trading.

All of the above are fairly major benefits and this list is not exhaustive. I think there is no limit to the benefits you may gain and a lot will depend on the way you trade.

Maybe the biggest benefit is that all of this is risk-free!

Are you a trader or gambler?

As a trader I have often been accused of being a gambler by friends and family. This is a charge I have hotly refuted.

At least up to now.

When I discovered binary bets and started to write about them (something I find very helpful in ordering my thoughts) I found that half the time I was talking about trading and the other half about betting. I know I have already touched on this point but this time the inference is different. I thought this through and came to the conclusion that betting and trading are very similar.

But generally a bet cannot be traded. Bets tend to be binding until the event is over. You bet on the 3:30pm at Sandown and you are stuck with that bet until the horses pass the winning post.

But with a trade you are free to close it whenever you like, as long as the market is open and subject to market rules.

A binary bet can be traded and thus I would tend to call it a *binary trade*. If we place a binary bet on the 3:30pm at Sandown and our horse leads the field for a while we may well close out at profit before the race is over.

This feature should be a revelation to those who bet on horses.

Similarly I have considered the meaning of the words *gambler* and *trader* and have come to the conclusion that there is very little difference in the vast majority of cases. But there is a huge difference between those who give themselves no real chance of success (whether trading or betting) and those who approach these activities as a business – I will call this latter group of people the *professionals*.

In this context I came across a highly amusing book recently called *The Man with the $100,000 Breasts and other gambling stories* by Michael Konik. The chapter about Brian Zembic and his 38C's is interesting enough but the chapter that particularly struck a chord is entitled "The World's Greatest Golf Hustler."

What I found so interesting were some of the quotes from Terrance Leon Jnr, the hustler in question, relating to his graduation from gambler to professional. Here are a few:

> "I was already making more money shooting pool (as a teenager) than I could ever make punching the time clock. Almost from the start I was a successful gambler. Only problem was I couldn't hold onto my money. I couldn't manage it right. I'd win eighty thousand playing nine-ball and turn right around and blow a hundred thousand on horses and sports. This went on for years."

Eventually, Leon decided to treat his gambling not as an addiction but as a business.

> "That's what made all the difference. Gambling stopped being fun and it started being a way to make a living. I figured I wasn't going to get involved in nothing unless I was getting the best of it. If I didn't have the advantage I wouldn't play. That's the secret. Find something where you are getting the best of the deal and stick with it until there ain't no money left to win."

If you want to find out exactly what Leon's edge is you will need to read the book. But we all need an edge and we all need to treat this as our business – *we need to get professional if we are to win.*

Playing the marble game is the kind of thing professionals do. Amateurs, otherwise known as gamblers, would probably not bother.

System Performance

The following charts are from a computerised version of this game (go to www.iitm.com for details) and the two charts below are based on the *same* system – you will notice a big difference in how it performed!

By using this computerised version you can very quickly run though a number of sequences that your system might produce. When trading a system mechanically the market becomes a generator of random sequences and, as I said earlier, these sequences will probe both yourself and your system for weaknesses.

By using this methodically you will be in a much better position to know what you can expect and you can also get a good handle on different money management techniques and how they will work in practice.

The two charts below are just two of a range of sequences but I thought you would be interested in seeing how different they are.

Chart 12.1: Sequence 1 – Wow – more of this please!

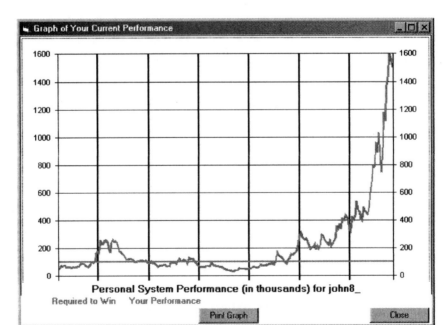

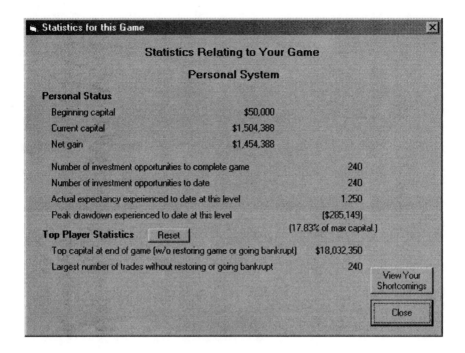

Statistics for this Game   [X]

Statistics Relating to Your Game

Personal System

Personal Status

Beginning capital	$50,000
Current capital	$1,504,388
Net gain	$1,454,388

Number of investment opportunities to complete game	240
Number of investment opportunities to date	240
Actual expectancy experienced to date at this level	1.250
Peak drawdown experienced to date at this level	($285,149)
	(17.83% of max capital.)

Top Player Statistics   [Reset]

Top capital at end of game (w/o restoring game or going bankrupt)	$18,032,350
Largest number of trades without restoring or going bankrupt	240

[View Your Shortcomings]

[Close]

Chart 12.2: Sequence 2 – Oh Dear! Better scrap this.

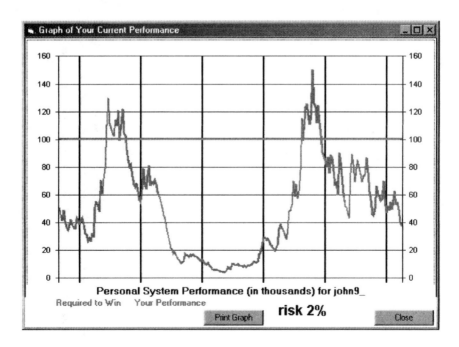

Graph of Your Current Performance   [_][□][X]

Personal System Performance (in thousands) for john9_

Required to Win   Your Performance   **risk 2%**

[Print Graph]   [Close]

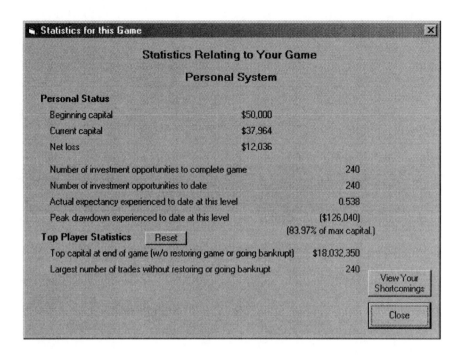

*Yes, I did say both these results were generated by the same system –
food for thought!*

Summary

In this chapter I introduce a simple game which may give you many
insights into your trading approach.

To play the game all you need is a number of different-coloured marbles
and an opaque bag.

13.

The Psychology of Trading the Binaries

In this chapter we are going to touch, briefly, on the key psychological elements that go towards making a winning binary trader and a winning system.

Binary bets may have some of the finest trading attributes I have ever seen, but you will still lose unless you pay due regard to the essentials in this chapter.

Some of the points mentioned below have been covered in earlier chapters and where this is the case I have summarised them below.

The Trading Pyramid

No book on betting or trading is complete without a mention of the following essential elements. Together these form the *Trading Pyramid*. They are:

1.   You

2.   Commitment

3.   Discipline

4.   Money Management

5.   Risk Control

6.   The Three Simple Rules

7.   System Parameters

8.   Your System/Methodology

9.   Operation

10. Profits/Losses

The order in which these are set out is also important. *You* form the base of the pyramid and each level must be in place and secure before the next level has a chance of functioning. Finally *Profits/Losses* determine how well you have built your pyramid and also determines the *Balance* which has to be inherent in your trading if you are to win.

Figure 13.1: The Trading Pyramid

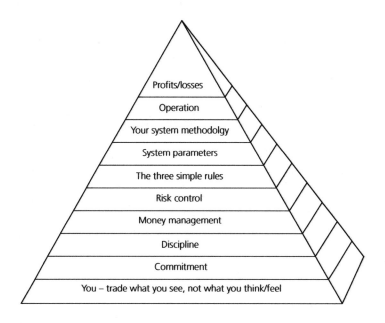

I will now give you a brief outline of each of these:

1. You

Clearly you need to be in place, both literally and metaphorically; otherwise nothing is going to happen. But you bring an awful lot of baggage with you when it comes to trading and betting. In particular, you are a bundle of emotions, instincts and thoughts. That is what makes us human and I would have it no other way. But markets tend to trigger different emotions and instincts and these all too easily make us abandon our system rules and make us place bets which we have no right to be taking at all. Such bets may even win following the principles of *random reinforcement* (which I discuss below under *discipline*). However, the habits produced by such behaviour are not winning habits and will eventually cost you dear.

Joe Ross said it best when he said:

Trade what you see, not what you think!

Build your system, and then trade following the rules based *on the market action you see.*

One of the key points about YOU and your emotions and instincts is that risk is something we deal with emotionally. It is all well and good working out our trading approach at an intellectual level but we will not be trading that much in that part of the brain.

2. Commitment

If you want to win you have got to be committed. Trading and betting are tough businesses. Of course you don't need to take it that seriously. Many get a lot of pleasure out of betting and trading, win or lose. The most important factor is not to risk more than you are *comfortable* losing. The word comfortable will mean many different things to different people. To some it will mean the cost of a few beers. Others will not be comfortable unless they feel *on edge* with a large amount at risk.

Don't be fooled into expecting easy money. Many people enter the arena thinking they are going to get rich without really trying and when they realise there is hard work involved they quit – better to realise this up front!

Having said that, I have found it much simpler to make money with binaries than with any other trading instrument I have ever come across. The longer-term bets I mentioned in earlier chapters can lend themselves to a particularly relaxed style of trading.

3. Discipline

To win you have got to formulate a winning approach. But it is not going to work very well unless you follow it. To do that requires discipline.

However, it goes beyond that as you will frequently find you are tempted to take non-system trades and break your rules on system trades. These are your emotions and instincts at play and they need to be kept in check.

To complicate the issue some of these random trades will make money. This is the concept of *random reinforcement* where we find that doing the *wrong* thing can reward us and doing the *right* thing can be punishing. In this way the situation can become confusing but if you have thoroughly tested your system you should know what is the right thing to do and, over time, you will develop the discipline to do it.

You, Commitment and Discipline are what you personally bring to the table. We now come on to the three principles behind all good trading.

4. Money management

Money management is a key concept. Bad money management can wipe you out more quickly than a bad trading system. Good money management can keep you safe in the worst conditions.

Money management dictates how much you risk on each bet. It is obvious that if you risk your entire account on every bet, you will be wiped out because no system has a 100% success rate. Even if the success rate is 99% (which it won't be) then that one bet will come along and wipe you out.

But if your system has a 50% success rate (which is far more likely) then statistically every 1000 bets you are going to hit a string of 10 or 11 losses. You will also hit a string of 10 or 11 profits but it is the losses we are concerned with here, because if you are trading in too big a size 10 or 11 losses will wipe you out. Given this statistic any risk above 5% of capital is likely to be deadly to you and this is why it is standard advice to risk no more than 1% or 2% on any one bet.

The amount that you should risk on any one bet will depend on your own system – whole books have been written about such calculations.

5. Risk control

Betting is a high-risk environment and to succeed you must adopt a low risk strategy. It is by using risk control that you do this. Risk control simply means adopting a number of strategies to keep a tight control on the risks you take.

Binary bets can do a lot of this automatically if you buy cheaply or sell at high prices. In both these cases the amount you risk on each bet will be a small number of points multiplied by the amount you bet per point. We have already discussed how much your total risk should be under *Money Management* above.

For my own trading I often takes these actions:

- I will reduce position size if time is passing and nothing is happening.
- I may halve my position in such a situation although this will depend on the prices available. I would not, for example, close at a price at which I would normally be delighted to open.

- I will also take profits early if time is running out rather than risking a reversal which may see a very sharp move against me. It is one of the characteristics of binary bets that as they near expiry they can become a lot more volatile.

6. The Three Simple Rules

You may have heard these before, they are:

1. Cut losses

2. Run profits

3. Trade selectively

Here is why these rules are so important:

- You have got to cut losses otherwise they will wipe you out.

- You have got to run profits otherwise you will never cover your losses.

- If you trade selectively you will only be taking the best opportunities and that will give you a decided edge.

(I look at these three rules in more detail in the next chapter.)

Money Management, Risk Control, and the Three Simple Rules are the guiding principles behind all trading and all system design. We now come to the results of these principles.

7. System parameters

These are the broad principles behind your betting system. They are the result of everything that has gone before and they are a reflection of your trading personality. They are based on your betting idea and incorporate the three simple rules.

8. Your system/methodology

This describes exactly the way in which you decide to trade. This is the result of all your testing as previously described. The system should be written down so that you know precisely what it is. Writing something down exerts a discipline and ensures, to an extent, that there is logic and clarity in what is written. This is particularly important when talking about trading systems.

The system should state what you look for when trading and your entry parameters. Especially regarding the price you are looking for, which in the case of a binary bet defines both your risk and your potential reward.

The system should further define your exit strategy and any proposed action to lock in profits or to take profits at certain levels and certain times.

Not all of this may be relevant. For example, a simple binary betting system may simply say, *buy bet X if it goes to 20 or less* and then let it run to expiry (in the hope that it may go to 100).

9. Operation

Operation may sound simple but it is not always so. With spread betting and binary betting it is all too easy to click the wrong button and find you have sold instead of bought. This can be fairly devastating; putting you into a high-risk position rather than the low-risk bet you had in mind.

But there can be more fundamental problems and some traders find they simply cannot push the button. There may be psychological reasons for this in which case there are consultants who can help or it may be an unconscious realisation that the system is, in reality, extremely high risk.

If the latter, then you need to go back and review your system and adjust it to overcome this problem.

Most people will be able to operate their system effectively but may encounter problems as success leads them to increase position size.

You are also likely to come across a very common problem which is over-confidence. It is a human trait to take full responsibility for all the good that happens to us but to blame others when things go wrong. This is one luxury a trader cannot afford.

Do not forget that your success is a direct result of all the work you have put in designing and testing your betting approach. Do not think that you are God's gift to the betting world and that you can now do exactly what you want with no regard to your system.

Don't laugh, as this is exactly what traders do.

They do well and get over confident. They abandon their rules and suffer heavy losses. They are then plunged into an abyss of fear and gloom which is not a good place to be when you are trying to make money. Over-confidence makes you abandon your system, fear and gloom make you excessively risk averse and so you do not give your bets room to breath as you are terrified of even the smallest loss.

Many traders spend their trading lives swinging between these two extremes. The trick is to realise what is happening and take avoiding action.

10. Profits/Losses

This is the final result of all your work. If you have built a well-balanced pyramid then you will be making profits. If your pyramid bears an uncanny resemblance to the leaning tower of Pisa then you will need to go back to the drawing board!

Summary

In this chapter we put in place a model which can prove extremely useful in helping you make money with binary bets. But the model also has wider applications and can be applied to most aspects of life.

When applied to binary bets the model has ten levels and these are:

- You
- Commitment
- Discipline
- Money Management
- Risk Control
- The Three Simple Rules
- System Parameters
- Your System/Methodology
- Operation
- Profits/Losses

These ten levels can also be characterised under these sub-headings:

1. **You and your psychology** (the first three)

2. **Money and risk** (the next three)

3. **Your system and using it** (the final four)

What the model tells us is that our psychology and the attention we pay to risk and money are at least as important as the betting itself. Get the foundations right and everything else becomes much more straightforward.

The Trading Pyramid is dealt with in more detail in my earlier book *The Way To Trade*.

14.

Binary Betting Rules

In this final chapter I am going to set out the key rules I believe you will need to follow if you are going to trade binary bets and win.

At the same time you can treat this chapter as a summary of the key features I have set out in this book.

Rule 1 – Control your losses

Whatever you bet or trade this is always rule one.

> Losses are inevitable and if you do not keep them under control then you will not come out on top – period!

I have explained how, when you trade the binaries your loss is always strictly limited. I have also explained that if you trade the binaries in such a way that you are always buying cheaply (i.e. below 40, or even better below 20), that you are automatically operating strict risk control.

I have said that an ideal ratio of average profit to average loss is 2.5 to 1. On this basis a good price to aim for is 28. If you buy a binary at 28, or sell at 72, then your risk is 28 points, £280 at £10 per point, and your potential profit is 72 points (100 – 28) or £720 at £10 per point. If you divide £720 by £280 you get 2.57. If you can find a bet you can buy at 28 and win half the time you will do very well!

I have also set out the fact that below 20 (or above 80 if selling binaries) binary prices tend to move quite slowly. This means that if you enter at these levels (or maybe at 28 which again scores on this point) you can exercise even tighter risk control and close a trade that looks to be going badly and then you may only lose half your intended stake.

But be warned – if you close in this way you will also be reducing your winners. Some of the trades which look hopeless will go on to win!

If you control your losers, it is said, the winners will look after themselves. This is true if you follow the next nine rules.

Rule 2 – Let your profits run

Human psychology is such that we tend to ignore losses and hope they will go away. In so doing we let them run. But if we see a profit we are so delighted that we grab it. In so doing we cut our profits.

Hence we lose.

To win we have to do the opposite, but it goes against many of our ingrained habits, habits based on our instincts and emotions. Habits built up over a lifetime.

There is a test that is given to children. They are left in a room with a single marshmallow and told if they do not eat it they will get two. Research has shown that those that have enough emotional control to delay eating that first marshmallow have a far better chance of winning in life (a higher proportion of girls pass that test!). Apparently this test is far more reliable than any number of IQ and other tests!

As traders we must learn to leave our initial profit alone so that it might grow into a multiple number of marshmallows.

As a rough guide it is essential that our average profit is at least twice our average loss. There are exceptions to this rule and one is where you are trading in a way which gives you a much higher proportion of winners, meaning well in excess of 50%. For example if 70% of your trades are winners then there is no reason why the amount you lose each time could not be the same as the amount you win, even a little more.

I need to make a final comment on the skill of running profits. It is primarily a passive skill, a skill of watching and taking no action. As such it is the complete opposite of cutting losses. Cutting losses is an active skill, one of watching, seeing and acting.

But a successful trader has to master both skills, two skills which are the complete opposite of each other. It is not so surprising that few make it.

This is where the unique features of binary bets come in – they can do the loss cutting bit automatically and allow you to concentrate on developing the skill to run profits. That alone makes a huge difference.

Rule 3 – Be selective – just bet ten times each year!

The first two rules define the essence of good trading. The third rule brings home the bacon, puts the icing on the cake and money in the bank. As you develop your approach to binary bets you will find certain opportunities which are particularly profitable and which are reliable.

Don't tell a soul!

Once you start talking about your best trades you will find they stop working and there is a very good reason for this. If you tell someone then they may well tell someone else and so it will spread. Once a number of traders start chasing the same idea you will find you cannot get the same prices either on entry or exit – the opportunity will vanish.

In trading, less is very much more. If you just take the best trades you will find your bottom line simply growing and growing. If you accept the dross as well you will find you just spin your wheels and maybe lose.

But this is no easy skill. Nor is it something you can do before you have developed your abilities. It does take a little experience to see which are the best trades. It also takes patience to wait for them.

Warren Buffett, and his partner Charlie Munger, suggest you should invest as if you can only make fifteen investments in your lifetime. The point being that if this were the case you would take great care and make sure they were excellent opportunities. If you applied a similar rule to your binary betting you may only find ten bets a year that meet your most exacting criteria. But if you just took those ten bets you would surely end up with more profit than if you took whatever came along.

Rule 4 – Bet at a comfortable size

This rule is all about how you feel. If you feel like a cat on a hot tin roof when you are placing bets then you are not going to win. If you feel frightened to death you are not going to win – scared money always loses.

The trick is to reduce the sums you are trading until you feel comfortable. In fact many people simply trade in too big a size in any case and good general advice is to halve your position size.

There is also Money Management to consider and if you trade in too large a size you will get wiped out – guaranteed. The fact that you would get wiped out is something you would probably realise, if only subconsciously, and that factor will make you feel even more uncomfortable.

The actual amount you feel comfortable with will vary from person to person and will also vary in direct relation to the capital you are trading. Personally, I increase the number of pounds per point as I win, and also reduce if I see losses.

Rule 5 – Understand the logic of your trading approach

In one very real sense the betting market is a generator of random sequences. This is particularly so when you use a precise trading methodology and, over time, the market will throw everything at your system that it can. If there is a flaw in the system the market will find it and exploit it to the maximum.

I will give you two examples:

1. If you are taking fairly high probability bets, perhaps buying at 60 or above leading you to expect to win on most of your trades, you will hit a string of losses far bigger than you expect. The laws of statistics guarantee this.

2. If you are using a risk control strategy whereby you buy at 60 but always get out if it goes down to 40 you will see trades where the market suddenly gaps and you get no chance to exit at 40. You will also see trades which go down to 40, you exit, and then they rapidly go up to 100.

This is another situation where binary betters are far better off than spread betters or futures traders. Because these instruments wear no corset they can move wherever they want and you can come badly unstuck in fast market conditions, especially if holding overnight – but binary bets keep you relatively safe whatever.

But you still need to understand the logic of your approach.

Rule 6 – Don't predict

I know many successful traders and none claim the ability to predict market action – I do not claim this myself. As a trader my function is to see good opportunities and take them. Some work out, some do not.

The point here is that it is important you do not get attached to your trades. If you start identifying with every trade and your self-esteem starts to depend on whether you are right or wrong then you will be on a slippery slope. There will always be losses and the mistake is not following your system – beat yourself up about that if you want.

I appreciate that there is an element of semantics in this. You might say if your trades have a 70% success rate, as they might well do if you are buying binaries at 60 plus, there is a prediction being made.

My own view is that you can only be said to predict anything if your hit rate is above 90% and that is never going to happen in the market.

Rule 7 – Don't panic

This one does not need much explanation and it will be fairly obvious that if you start to panic you are liable to make all the wrong choices. But if you follow rules 4 and 5 you should never get into that position. It is only when your positions are too large and/or when you are hit by something you did not expect that there is any danger of this.

I do have personal experience of this which came about neither because I did not understand the logic of my system nor because I was over-trading but simply because my funds grew substantially and I was suddenly trading in much greater size (over $1m). To my surprise I found this brought on a panic attack. Thankfully it only happened once and I was fine afterwards – but it is something to bear in mind.

Again the characteristics of binary bets protect you from the most obvious problems but if you overtrade and take large risks then panic may be your constant companion.

Rule 8 – Stay humble/balanced – big egos are expensive to run

This can be tough as the megabucks roll in but it is essential. I speak to many traders and they all say the same thing

I was doing so well and then...

Yes, it all went wrong because they became arrogant and over-confident.

The problem with arrogance is that you are so full of yourself that there is no room for anything else. In this state you cannot learn and one thing you need to do in markets is learn.

Rule 9 – Find a trading mentor

This is an important one.

You will save yourself a lot of heartache and a lot of time if you can find someone to help you through the early stages. It always surprises me that more traders do not do this. Betting and trading are not easy yet most people just leap in regardless.

I accept that there is no obvious route to take but many traders would be happy to help out if asked. I am not guaranteeing this but most traders I have spoken to do say that the idea appeals to them. I take on consultancy clients and I find that I often learn much from these clients, so it is a two-way process. When you start to teach something you are forced to know what you are talking about.

Rule 10 – Betting can be a lot of fun, but if you want to win treat it seriously

This may be the most important of the ten rules for winning.

Too many traders treat it all like a game but if you want to win you need to treat it very, very seriously. As with any business you need a plan. The Appendix provides a plan which may give you a template to work to. But do not get too fixated on doubling at regular intervals. If you are just starting out you have got to learn the basics before you can fly. With binary bets there is a lot less to learn than with other trading vehicles but that does not mean it is going to be easy. You also need to plan your trading and Chapter 9 provides a way in which you can do this.

You also need to plan yourself and the trading pyramid as outlined in Chapter 11 should be a big help.

Finally be sure to become an expert in your chosen trading/betting approach.

Do the research.

15.

The Beginning

It may seem odd to call the final chapter *the beginning* but, if a book is any good, it is a door into a new world.

Some who read this book will be inspired to pit their wits in the binary betting arena and some will build a new and better life for themselves by doing so. For them this is indeed the beginning.

Others will take what I have said and incorporate some of my techniques into their own trading and/or simply use them for the occasional flutter.

In this chapter I want to suggest an approach to the material herein to maximise the benefits to you.

I have included separate chapters on these three techniques:

- Trading the news
- Trading the waves
- Trading the spikes

In previous chapters I also introduced trendlines and options expiry as additional techniques.

I will use *trading the news* to illustrate these points but they apply equally to every one in this book.

Here is my suggested approach:

1. Read the chapter a few times to make sure you are totally familiar with the material

2. Then start to look at these signals in real life.

3. Make sure you look at both the market action and the binary betting prices.

4. With news you have the satisfaction of getting immediate gratification (or not).

5. Paper trade these events a few times so that you have clear record of what happened and make notes.

6. Study all the possible permutations involved. For example the perceived importance of the news and the relative position of the market to parity when it comes out.

7. Watch the action after the news and how the binary betting prices behave.

8. Extend my comments and develop your own modifications.

9. As you continue to trade your experience will grow.

10. You will then become the *expert* (and perhaps I will have the pleasure of reading your book on the subject at some point in the future!)

Change

But we also need to look at a final point which will have big effect on your success or failure as a trader.

I am talking about change – because change is the only thing that is guaranteed in the markets. As I write this the betting companies do not factor in the volatility that may be seen once news comes out – and this is why the news gives us a good trading opportunity.

If lots of people start to position ahead of the news then this will change and the price may go too far the other way – it may pay to buy/sell bets that would benefit if there is only a muted reaction to the news.

Your expertise will still be useful but you will need to apply it differently.

> I often talk about building on rock, not sand. If you put in the work then what you learn will be solidly based and stand you in good stead for the future.

Good luck!

It only remains for me to wish you the very best of luck. But if you follow these guide lines you should not need it!

I always appreciate feedback and feel free to email me on john@john-piper.com with any comments you might have. As comments and questions come in I plan to build a *knowledge base* on www.johnpiper.info

Appendices

I

Directory of Binary Betting Companies

Here is a list of those companies offering binary bets at this time.

IG Index – www.igindex.com

Capital Spreads – www.capitalspreads.com

Binary bets – www.binarybet.com

Finspreads – www.finspreads.com

City Index – www.cityindex.com

Cantor Index – www.cantorindex.co.uk

BetOnMarkets – www.BetOnMarkets.com

BetsForTraders – www.BetsForTraders.com

Betfair – www.Betfair.com

HedgeStreet Inc – www.hedgestreet.com

Of these final two BetFair is a fixed-odds betting exchange offering bets in decimal format in the main. HedgeStreet is a US binary site which was recently bought by IG Index.

Cash from the betting companies

It is one of the features of binary betting that the betting companies are so keen to have you sign up as a client that they will give you cash to do so. They do this because they expect to make money from you – why else? The whole purpose of this book is to reverse this process and help you to make money from them.

To give you a head start in this process we set out below some of the companies that are offering cash at this time.

Note: these offers change all the time so it may pay to check out the company website to see whether you can find something better!

- **BetsForTraders** – www.BetsForTraders.com
  £100 will be credited to your account immediately you deposit £200 but withdrawal restrictions apply. To receive this make sure you enter the promotional code JPB100.

- **BetOnMarkets** – www.BetOnMarkets.com
  £20 will be credited to your account on opening and to get this add the promotional code JP888 at the appropriate point in the application form. No deposit is necessary with this offer.

- **Capital Spreads** – www.capitalspreads.com
  £75 will be credited to your account after you have made two non-equity bets as long as you deposit at least £250. Withdrawal restrictions apply. To obtain this make sure you say you were introduced via "John Piper".

Be sure to check out the terms and conditions before signing up. You often have to jump through a few hoops to get this cash.

At the time of going to press most of these offers for readers of this book were better than the offers on the websites and you will need to log in as stated above to obtain these figures.

If you want regular updates on the offers available together with a quick link to the betting companies and the full terms and conditions of these offers then simply send a blank email to freetrades@aweber.com

II

Futures, Options and Binary Bets

I mentioned earlier in the book that the two main forms of betting were fixed-odds and spread betting. It is interesting to briefly mention the relationship between betting and the financial markets of futures and options.

- **Futures** have similarities with spread betting.
- **Options** combine some of the aspects of fixed-odds betting with some of the characteristics of spread betting. When you buy an option all you can lose is your stake (just liked fixed-odds betting), but your reward is theoretically unlimited (just like spread betting). You can also sell options in which case your reward is limited to the premium received, but your risk is theoretically unlimited.

For those of you who have had experience of other trading vehicles I set out below the characteristics of binary bets compared to futures and options – these are the factors that attracted me to binary bets in the first place. Attractive features of binary bets:

1. The ability to enter at a low price (15 or less) which amounts to your total risk.
2. The possibility of 6x profit from such a position.
3. The possibility of a large gain from a very small move.

Options offer the first but rarely the second. Futures can offer the second, but rarely, and risk is greater. Neither futures nor options offer the third.

But there are always pros and cons and with binary bets the biggest downside is that the binary price that is available when you want to trade may not be that good. For example, if your indicators show an uptrend but the binary bet is already up at 75/80 it may be seen as a high risk bet with limited potential – but this need not be the case. If your approach has a very high success rate then you might find a price of 75/80 very acceptable. Alternatively, other binaries, such as a OneTouch, may give a better price.

The other disadvantage is timescale, as most binary bets are only suitable for short-term trading. The exception are the bets offered by www.BetOnMarkets.com and www.BetsForTraders.com

---

The key feature of a binary bet – that differentiates it from other trading vehicles – is that, traded correctly, it offers a built in low-risk opportunity.

III

Answers to Exercises

Answers to questions raised in the section *Research* in Chapter 2.

When I did this exercise I found that the Dow will move 100 points or more away from the prior close approximately 25% of the time. The reverse side of this coin is that the Dow will stay within a 100/100 Tunnel 75% of the time.

If we narrow the range to 60 points then my research showed that the Dow will stay within a 60/60 Tunnel just 35% of the time.

This information should be useful but it would be far more useful if you did the research yourself and, in particular, directed your research to particular trading areas that interest you. If you want to win then it is important you treat your trading and betting as a business. Good businessmen and women do their research carefully and diligently.

For this reason I have not given further answers to this exercise.

In addition, if you decide to trade in this way you will need to give thought to how often the Dow will gap open and thus disrupt these simple statistics.

I will add that I did this initial research early in 2007 and these percentages changed quite a lot as markets became more volatile later that year and in 2008. This underlines the importance of doing research yourself as you need to be able to adapt as conditions change. See Chapter 10 for more on this topic.

IV

The 5 Point Trading System

I want to introduce a trading plan.

This particular plan is pretty powerful stuff, although it may seem far fetched. It may seem impossible. It may be impossible! But it does provide a plan, and a plan is always useful.

First, a simple question.

How many points do you think you could take out of the market every day of the week?

When I ask people this question they tend to say 10, 20 or perhaps even more. Well it's nice to dream but why not settle for just 5 points a day from FTSE, the Dow or any binary bet? Does that seem unreasonable?

Well, with just 5 points a day you will rule the world!

I introduced this concept back in 1992. At that time the FTSE futures traded at £25 per point and you needed margin of £2500. But now you can start spread betting with as little as £100. What is more the margin requirement on a binary bet is the maximum you can lose – as little as £5, £10 or £20 on certain bets. There are betting companies allowing you to trade in pennies, with these we can further reduce these figures.

The point is that if you can just make 5 points every day you will be a millionaire 15 months from now.

Here's how.

1. There are usually around 20 trading days in a month.

2. You make 5 points each day clear of the spread.

3. You open your account with just £100 and bet just £1 per point.

4. Each month you bring in 100 points – 5 points each day for 20 days, 5 x 20 – that is £100 in month 1. At the end of the first month you have doubled your money – that may not seem very exciting with just £100, but wait, you will get all the excitement you want before too long.

5. For the second month you trade £2 per point. Again you go for just 5 points a day, on average.

6. Each month you double your money. At the end of six months you have £3200, at the end of a year you have £204,800; and you are trading over £2000 per point – enough excitement for you?

7. Two months later and you have over £800,000 and easily top £1m a week or so later.

What's to stop you?

Here is a list:

- **Consistency**
  This is your biggest stumbling block.

- **Losses**
  Which are going to set you back.

- **Complacency**
  Having attained wealth you will lose your hunger and the risks will no longer seem worthwhile.

- **Market limitations**
  Spread betting companies have limits on bet sizes of £100 and above per bet, but you are allowed more than one bet at that limit. Plus there are a number of spread betting companies. Nevertheless larger bet sizes will cause problems.

Now let's get real

The idea of doubling your money every month is a nice fairy tale – and it almost makes sense but I have skipped over the flaws. However there is a lot of real sense in this fairy tale, so now let's adapt it for the real world.

Firstly let's consider money management and in particular how this is going to affect the majority of people. The idea of looking for very small, short-term profits (i.e. 5 points on a binary bet, half a point on the S&P, 5 points on FTSE or the Dow), can work although you would need to apply correspondingly close stops for risk control. In all trading you must either look for bigger profits than the losses you are prepared to accept or you need to use an approach which offers a high percentage of winning trades – over 70%. There are certain strategies using binary bets which do offer that sort of percentage.

For this sort of trading you would need to watch the markets very closely. You may decide you would rather trade in a more relaxed style. That is also fine. But to do this you may need to increase your starting capital.

So what about losses?

Clearly these are going to set you back – but, as long as your money management is effective, only in the way of time. As long as your trading methodology is effective and you do make progress then this process will work for you.

Guidelines

It might be useful to put forward some guidelines. So here goes.

- Don't bump up your initial trading size in relation to your cash. There is no point – if this works you will soon be trading more than enough contracts.

- Don't rush increasing position size. You have to be prudent – that is the key to handling all risk. It is when risk is allowed to run out of hand that it becomes dangerous.

- If you find that the size you are trading is making you nervous, drop down a little to your comfort zone. Nervous money never wins!

Here are a couple of other points:

- You can increase position size other than by doubling each time. You could adopt an approach based on a percentage of your trading capital – in fact this may help with nervousness as you would be gradually increasing as you win – and gradually decreasing as losses come in.

- The market does provide a number of opportunities for taking small quick profits. In particular, support or resistance points usually produce at least a tradeable reaction, especially if the market is oversold or overbought at that point.

In life there is one great truth (among others): this is that a man with a plan has a march on the no-plan man. So why not think about how this process could be applied to your trading.

V

Stops and Limits

These are terms from the financial world, not the betting world, and need some explanation.

Limits

A limit means that you will only enter or exit a position at a certain price or better.

To give an example, you may want to buy the *FTSE to end up* bet. The current price is 32/36 but you only want to pay 25. You would be very happy to pay less than 25 and any price below 25 would be "better" for you.

So you enter a *limit* to buy this bet at 25 or better. If the price touches 25 you will have placed the bet. The "or better" bit is good in theory but in practice does not happen with binary bets. In fact very few betting companies have this facility and when they do it does not seem to work too well.

However this may change and whenever I meet with one of these companies I always urge them to introduce limits. So far my suggestions are being considered but no more than that.

Nevertheless this might change and I will just explain a little more about limits and how you can also exit a position using them.

In the example above we placed a limit to buy the bet *FTSE to end up* at 25. We will now assume that the price went below 25 and we placed the bet at 25. We now decide that we would be happy to sell at 75 or better. So we place another limit to sell on that basis. If the price touches or goes above 75 we will sell at 75 for a profit of 50 points (75 minus 25).

As I said above very few companies allow you to use limits at all and those that would allow you to place the first limit would not allow the second. However you can get round this if you are using a bet which has a pair.

Bet pairs

An example of a pair of bets are *FTSE to end up* and *FTSE to end down*. We discussed this in Chapter 2 as complementary or mirror bets.

To return to our example we have placed a limit at 25 or better and bought the *FTSE to end up* bet at 25. Our betting company, unusually, allows us to place limit orders to open but not to close. But if we place a limit to buy the *FTSE to end down* bet and if that price is hit we will end up with a pair of bets which, in effect, cancel each other out. There is a complete example of this in Chapter 2.

We want to sell our bet at 75 and selling *FTSE to end up* for 75 is equivalent to buying *FTSE to end down* at 25. So we place a second limit to buy *"FTSE to end down"* at 25 or better.

If limits are available then you should be able to place a limit to sell as well as buy a bet and it is important to note that the "or better" when selling means a higher price although as I have noted above this is unfortunately academic.

If we had simply sold the bet at 75 our profit would have been 50. By placing the limit on the second bet we are in the same position. Here is how it works out:

- If **FTSE ends up** we have a profit of 75 on *FTSE to end up* being 100 less 25. We also have a loss of 25 on our second bet *FTSE to end down*. The profit of 75 less the loss of 25 equals 50.

- If **FTSE ends down** we have a loss of 25 on *FTSE to end up* being zero less 25. We also have a profit of 75 on our second bet *FTSE to end down* being 100 less 25. The profit of 75 less the loss of 25 equals 50.

Finally if our second limit is not hit and we never buy the second bet at 25 we are again in the same position in that we simply lose the 25 put down on the first bet.

IG Index do offer an alert service which will send alerts to your mobile or by email and by using this you can at least get a warning if the market is at a point of interest. You cannot use this on the binary bets themselves, and it is not actually a limit, but by setting an alert on the underlying market you are achieving the next best thing.

We will now look at stops.

Stops

A stop is a way of limiting your risk. If you buy at a price, say 35, then a stop would be an order to exit at, say 20. It would seek to get you out with a smaller loss than the entire sum originally staked.

Let me give you an example based on the bet *FTSE 6220 OneTouch* which was part of the detailed example given earlier. In the example this bet was originally sold at 43. Half of the bet was then bought back at 62.2 and the other half went to expiry at 100 – a loss in both cases and the total loss amounted to £381.

If we had placed a stop at 70 the situation would have been different. Firstly it is less likely we would have closed at 62.2 as we would have let the stop do its job. Thus once the binary reached 70 we would have been stopped out. It is important to note that whereas limits have a theoretical *"or better"* stops have a very real *"or worse."*

Therefore although we may place a stop at 70 it is quite likely that it will be exercised at 72 or maybe 76. But even at 76 this is better than letting the loss run to close at 100. If the entire £10 per point were closed at 76 the total loss would be £330 (76 less 43 at £10 per point). Still considerably less than the loss in the example at £381.

Summary

- For **buy orders**: limit [stop] levels are always set below [above] the current market price.

- For **sell orders**: limit [stop] levels are always set above [below] the current market price.

How betting companies regard limits and stops

However, the discussion of stops is rather academic as none of the betting companies provide stops. This may change but I do not think it is likely as stops present a serious problem to the betting companies. Limits are a different matter as the punter is saying "yes, please get me in/out at this level of my choice." But with a stop the punter is saying "OK, I want to limit my risk but I don't want to get stopped out and would much rather see the bet go to a profit."

This presents a fairly big problem for the betting companies as punters can get disgruntled if they lose money and it is the nature of binary betting prices that their calculation is complex. There are known factors such as time and price but there are also variables such as volatility which can be calculated in a number of different ways. Another factor that can affect price is the weight of money and any bookmaker will want to balance his book where there is an excess of cash riding on one side of a bet.

The result of this complexity is that it can prove difficult to justify a particular price at any one time. The betting companies prefer to avoid the situation where they have an angry punter at one end of the phone who has just been stopped out of a position which would have gone on to win £1200. Explanations about arcane volatility calculations and the behaviour of the VIX (an index of volatility) are likely to fall on deaf ears in such a situation.

My view is that the betting companies are right not to allow the use of stops for these reasons. But it is different with a limit because the punter *wants* the limit to be exercised. Plus if the trade is a loser the punter cannot complain because the limit would *always* have been exercised as the price moved through the limit and beyond. Conversely if the trade is a winner who is going to complain? Celebrate maybe, but not complain!

Personally I would not use stops with binary bets but I do scale down position size where the odds start to turn against me. For example if nothing is happening and time is dwindling away I might close half my positions.

VI

Market Profile and Minus Development

The following is an extract from my first book, *The Way to Trade* (gratefully used with permission).

Market Profile

Market Profile (MP) is a method of organising market information into a format more useful to those who wish to profit from trading markets. Peter Steidlmayer discovered this approach and his genius was simple, he brought the age-old statistical tool, the bell curve, to bear on the market. The bell curve has always been something of a magician. It may not turn lead into gold, but does turn chaos into order. Some may say this is a more impressive feat.

Fig 18.1 Chaos into order

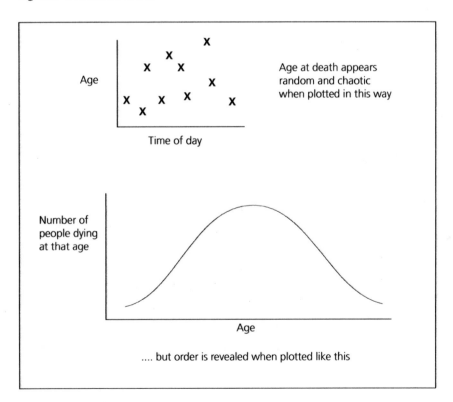

Perhaps death is the best example.

Look at a range of individuals and how death strikes may appear fairly random, as do heights, size of feet, etc. But take large numbers and then we find that we have a normal distribution – a bell curve. Few at the extremes and many in the middle. So is often the case with markets.

There is a certain amount of jargon associated with MP which may not be familiar to some traders. I will now seek to explain some of this jargon.

Traders often speak of *trending* and *non-trending* markets. Market Profile uses similar, but different, concepts, these being *balance* and *imbalance*.

As cash comes in or goes out of the market (from the actions of the longer time frame buyer or seller) this causes sharp price moves – and this action is referred to as *imbalance*. The market then has to digest this action and *balance* takes place.

Within the profile for each session similar concepts are *development* and *minus development* (MD). I define development as consisting of at least three TPOs (Time Price Opportunities) thick. MD as two or less (see Figure 18.2).

TPOs are the building blocks of Market Profile and each price appearing within a 30-minute price segment is a TPO. So MD means that price has spent an hour or less at that price, development occurs when price has spent an hour or more at that level. In a typical profile MD occurs at the extremes and development in the middle (see Figure 18.3).

If we were to look at a profile of people's heights we would note that there were not many people who were less than 3 feet high, nor many larger than 7 feet. In the market the action within a particular session often forms a bell curve which is the classic *Market Profile* form. Where the action is fast there is no development and hence we have the term *Minus Development* (MD).

Fig 18.2 The bell curve and TPOs

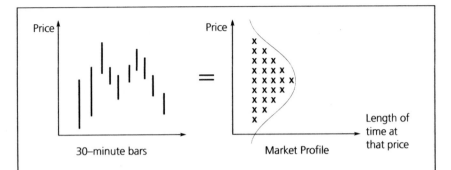

Note: each price on each 30–minute bar is represented by an "X" (a TPO). These are then used to compile the market profile chart. Such charts normally use different letters to mark each different 30–minute segment. I have not done this so as to simplify the presentation.

Fig 18.3 The bell curve

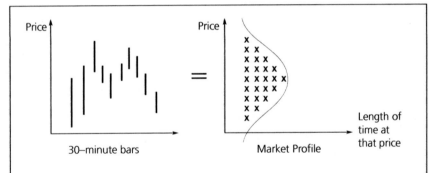

Note: each price on each 30–minute bar is represented by an "X" (a TPO). These are then used to compile the market profile chart. Such charts normally use different letters to mark each different 30–minute segment. I have not done this so as to simplify the presentation.

Minus Development

MD comes in a variety of forms and is an important concept for MP. Indeed it is about the only aspect of MP that I use.

Most commonly it is fast action being formed of no more than two TPOs (see below) whether such action is seen at the extreme of a day's price range (spikes) or whether bell curves form at either end. But it also means gaps (the ultimate minus development) and levels where the market does not go (i.e. a strong resistance level established over a number of time periods). In this way MD is a fairly broad concept and it might be said that MD gives traders the reference against which to measure their trades. Certainly MD provides indications for stop levels.

Value

Perhaps the central feature of MP is the concept of value. This concept is fairly unique in technical analysis to MP – surprisingly so given its importance.

When you know where value lies you know that to sell above it or to buy below – it gives you a much needed edge. There is, of course, nothing fixed about value and any attempt to be too scientific is bound to fail. Statistically 66% of a range of items falls within one standard deviation (SD) from the mean. This is how MP gauges value, it is the price range one SD either side of the mean within any session, or larger group of sessions.

Earlier I referred to TPOs. Each entry on a MP chart is a TPO (see Figure 18.4), and the reason for the name is obvious, each entry is a Time Price Opportunity.

Fig 18.4 Minus Development

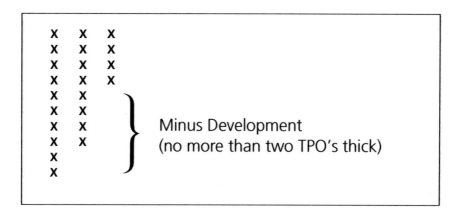

MP is fractal in that it can be applied successfully across a range of different time frames. It seems to be true that the longer the time frame the more reliable the results, and the shorter the time frame the more inconsistent.

This brings us to one of the primary approaches that can be utilised from this form of analysis.

First I must say that it is an approach of the utmost simplicity – but then this is true of most things which work well.

The strategy is simple: look for a signal from the longer time frame (the monthly profiles) and then wait for the shorter term to fall into place. Thus when entering a trade we may look to get an edge on value not only in the short term but also the longer term.

This produces the rationale that unless the trade goes right almost immediately we do not stay with it. But we do not need to – because there are quite enough which do go right.

The key to any trading success is taking low risk opportunities. Risk can only be defined if you know what to do if things go wrong. My methodology uses MD to define its trades. I utilise three types of exit approach:

1. First a money management stop is placed at a place where I would not expect the market to go (i.e. beyond normative rotational behaviour).

2. Second, I place a warning level either at or beyond MD and if price is accepted at that level I get out. The concept of *price acceptance* may be unfamiliar, but essentially if development forms at a level, price is accepted (see Chapter 15 of TWTT). Non-acceptance of price is perhaps an easier concept and a spike is an example of this.

3. The third approach is to simply exit if the market does not do as expected. When I enter I am looking for an opportunity available to few traders, if price is subsequently accepted at that level it is a negative and so often I will simply get out.

Once a trade is in profit similar approaches are adopted.

Other concepts

There are a few other concepts which you need to be aware of.

The *Initial Balance* (IB) is the price range during the time taken for the market to find a fair price, defined as where two-way trading takes place. Usually this takes about an hour but for some markets this may be longer or shorter.

Range Extension (RE) is movement beyond this IB (see Figure 18.5). Such movement may either be initiative or responsive depending where value lies in relation to that day's trading. Generally if buyers come in at the low end of value this is termed responsive (i.e. buyers are responding to the attractive prices). However, if sellers were to come in instead this would be initiative (i.e. sellers initiating further downwards action at unattractive prices). The opposite applies at the high end of value.

Fig 18.5 Initial Balance and Range Extension

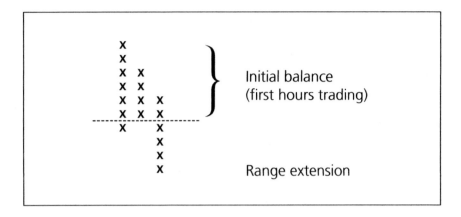

The previous day's value, or *Value Area* (VA), IB, RE, responsive and initiative action, all act as indicators of what is happening in the market and give clues as to what the longer time frame trader is doing. Referring back to the start of this piece, the action of the longer time frame trader is what drives directional moves in the market.

TTT article

The following appeared in *TTT* early in 1998 (there is some duplication but new ideas are often best assimilated if explained more than once in different ways):

For some months we have been working with an institutional trader ("IT"). This trader has impeccable credentials and has been consistently profitable over the last five years and made significant profits in 1994 when many professionals fared badly. His style of trading is what we might term relaxed. He is looking to catch the intermediate swings and so, on FTSE, he may just trade two or three times a month. But when he does so he is looking to catch significant moves. This is a style of trading I know many readers would wish to emulate and the following is designed to set out the methodology of this trader but also to say a few words about another approach to success in the markets.

Trading is all about finding and taking low risk opportunities. To find these opportunities our IT uses Market Profile (MP), which is a way of displaying historic market action to highlight such opportunities.

Before we go into greater detail we must say that MP is a subject about which books have been written. The purpose of this piece is to allow readers to understand the basis of the methodology used and a way of trading using MP.

MP is an alternative method of charting historic price action which might therefore be compared to methods such as bar charts, point and figure charts and candlesticks. It differs from these others in that the day is divided into time segments. Initially 30-minute segments were used but this has now been expanded and traders can use whatever segments suit them. Each segment is then plotted against a vertical price scale in the same way as a bar chart except that the price segments are squeezed into the vertical axis.

For example, if the opening segment sees prices between 3100 and 3110 then this will be marked on the chart. If the next segment trades between 3095 and 3105 then the action between 3095 and 3099 inclusive will be marked on the same vertical line as for the first segment and the action between 3100 and 3105 inclusive will be marked alongside the first segment. In this way a profile is built up for each day's action which often resembles a bell curve (see Figures 18.6 and 18.7).

The profile gives further information about market action and in particular can be used to express value. This is important because, as traders, we want to enter trades offering low risk opportunities. A definition of such an opportunity might be to sell above value and to buy below value. Because the profile shows value it therefore provides just such opportunities.

Value is calculated as the price action within one standard deviation of the mean on each day and value can be expressed as a bid/offer spread. However we need to expand on the expression mean. MP uses *Time Price Opportunities* (TPOs) and each tick on an MP chart is such a TPO. To put this another way, within each time segment there will be a certain price range and each price within this range will form a tick and therefore a TPO. It is the mean of all these TPOs which gives rise to the calculation of value.

Fig 18.6 Bar chart

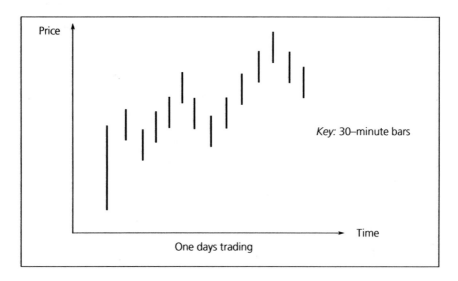

Fig 18.7 MP chart

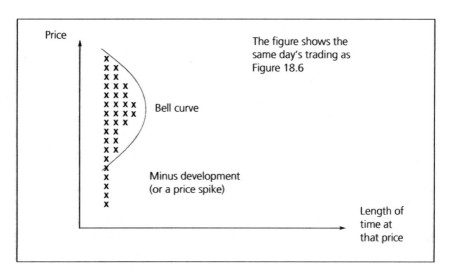

Another way of putting this, and this can be said to be the underlying principle behind MP, is:

> **Price over Time = Value**

Or, alternatively, Price through Time reveals Value.

To understand this statement is not easy, indeed I still have a few problems with it myself, but it does go to the root of this effective technique. In the main it refers to the amount of time for which a particular price is traded during a session.

Once value has been established from the profile of a day's trading it is then important to read the subsequent action. For example, if the market quickly falls back and thus rejects the bid that is a sign of weakness, but it is not necessarily useful because we want to sell at the offer not the bid (i.e. we want to sell above value). So an ideal trade would be if the subsequent day we saw a move up to the offer price and then a quick rejection of that level with the market falling back.

If we see such action then we have the opportunity of selling above value confirmed by the quick rejection of those prices. It is precisely such situations which a good trading system may be designed to capture. Both selling above value and buying below value.

You will see from this that MP is neutral of the market. By this we mean that as you look at a day's profile you do not know whether the following day will provide a low risk buying or selling opportunity.

But other techniques used by the IT do give a directional bias.

One of these is consensus theory. Our trader has built up a large network of market traders and advisers who regularly feed him information. This allows him to form a view on the consensus and if one becomes clear he is on the alert to go in the other direction. He finds this one of his most reliable indicators. Another is the long-term trendlines which we occasionally publish in *TTT*. When the market is at an extreme, either way, then he knows that an excellent low risk opportunity may be at hand.

So although MP is the motor which drives his methodology there are other techniques which hone it. Also there is a body of money management, risk control, discipline, stress management, etc. backing up the methodology itself.

Chaos makes the new possible, that is its significance

James Sloman, *Nothing*

Trading tips with Market Profile

In our work we often come across successful traders but when we analyse what they do we find that they just select a few core ideas and use those. As such they may believe that they are "Elliott," "Gann," "Market Profile," or "Wave" specialists, but in fact they are not, they just take a few good ideas and use them to their advantage, and they become expert on these.

Incidentally I have never met a pure "Elliott" or "Gann" specialist who is a successful trader – think about it. I believe that Gann and Elliott can be the most misleading techniques in the market today (and it is unclear whether Gann ever made a fortune trading). This is not to knock Elliott or Gann's work, merely the hype surrounding it. Nor is my purpose to knock any other forms of analysis, it is to show how MP can be used to make money. The following ideas are useful:

- The concept of value, as previously discussed, allows beneficial trade location in whatever time frame.

- The concept of MD is useful for the purposes of trading reference.

- Some of the strategies set out in Chapter 22 of *The Way to Trade* are based entirely around MD.

For the purposes of trend following MP has a number of advantages to offer. These can be summarised in the fact that it is only if initiating action against the trend is seen that the trend must be called into question. Further such action which is swiftly rejected is not conclusive (i.e. the initiating action has to be accepted). Thus MP allows a fairly sophisticated trend following approach.

Summary

- The magic of the bell curve turns Chaos into Order.

- Balance and imbalance are Market Profile terms which correspond with non-trending and trending markets.

- Minus development is a key technique of Market Profile which I use every day in my own trading.

- The value area is a central feature of Market Profile although I find I use this less than Minus Development.

- When trading I use primarily three types of exit. First, a money management stop which is a fair way away. Second, a closer level, normally beyond Minus Development, where I may exit depending on market action. Third, a quick exit if I do not immediately get the action I expect.

- Initial balance and range extension are two additional Market Profile concepts I use.

- Price over time is one of the underlying principles of Market Profile and refers to the amount of time at which the market traded at a particular price within a trading session.

VII

LunchTime Trader and JPT

When I write a book my aim is always to help traders, and those who want to become traders, to make money in the market. Although an important starting point is to keep losses small.

Similarly my trading services are designed to the same end. When it comes to learning the essentials there is nothing better than a good book or seminar but you also need practice dealing with the "right hand side" of the chart – meaning the part you cannot see yet because it hasn't happened.

In this book I have taken you through a number of real life trading situations and backed this up by the commentary I wrote at the time. In some cases you will also find video clips on my website – www.johnpiper.info – some of them recorded in real time as the trades unravel.

In life it is all too easy to reconstruct the past and having access to my comments at the time gives you a warts and all view of how it really happened, unaffected by the events that transpired.

If you are interested in either of my services then my website has full details but here is a quick résumé:

JohnPipersTrading (JPT)

Subscribers to JPT get my monthly newsletter (*The Technical Trader*), a weekly video clip of markets "tomorrow," and two reports daily picking out the trading opportunities on FTSE, the Dow, the DAX, the Nikkei Dow, Gold and T-Bonds. The 10:00am report includes *the chart of the day*. The price is £112.25 per quarter and new subscribers also get a free copy of my best-selling book *The Way to Trade*.

LunchTime Traders (LTT)

LTT is a more focused service and is dedicated to binary betting with precise recommendations. Reports are issued daily and often a bet is recommended. The *TradeWatch* section has been particularly successful and this focuses on bets I expect to give good profit potential and allows subscribers to choose their own entry point. Subscription costs £223.75 per quarter and comes with a full one month money-back guarantee.

Index

C

D

S

T

W

V